I0462783

Retirement Income Strategy If Financial Planning Is Not Enough

How to Retire 2019 Passive Income Strategies for Beginners: Airbnb Business, Freelancing, Dropshipping, Facebook & Instagram Marketing

Table of Contents

Introduction

Congratulations on downloading this book, and thank you for doing so.

Sarah Carter Crews and her husband have been small business owners, and she has been a health care provider and employee over her lifetime. They raised a large family of successful kids on a shoestring budget and enjoyed traveling and camping with the kids.

Facing retirement with minimal savings, they realized that they would not be able to financially cope if they did not come up with ways to earn passive income. One thing they did know for sure was that they did not want to spend the rest of their days continually worried and stressed about their finances every month. They decided to get creative and reinvent their skills to develop several streams of passive income. First, they listed their spare space in their home on Airbnb and VRBO and used their skills to develop several other streams of passive income, which gradually built momentum and success over time.

They now enjoy time with their grandkids and supplement their social security to give them the life and freedom they desired. By freeing up most of their time, they can travel, go on occasional cruises, camp and see the country.

Sarah and her husband knew that there were more people out there who shared their dreams. Dreams of traveling the world and spending more time with their friends and family once they stop working too. However, most people will not been able to save enough to stop having a stable income. It is estimated that one in three Americans have next to no retirement savings at all, and with the current cost of living and standard income rates, it is almost impossible to save up for retirement. Experts say that people will need a nest egg of over $1 million to last them through a 30-year retirement. *Even* then, that may not even be enough.

Are you preparing to retire soon, or already envisioning life after retirement? It is not too late and never too early to begin planning for it. We decided to team up with Sarah and her husband to create this book, providing a step-by-step guide on how you can survive retirement with little or no savings! They want the world to know that they are *living proof* that you can still generate a passive income stream, and live your retirement dreams the way you have always wanted. *Even* without having enough money saved. *It is still possible* and what you're about to discover here is going to change your financial worries forever. In a world full of options, there is always a way to make something happen.

There are plenty of books on this subject on the market, thanks again for choosing this one! Every effort was made to ensure it is full of as much useful information as possible. Please enjoy! After listening to or reading this book an honest review is greatly appreciated!

Chapter 1: The Retirement Mindset

Ah, retirement; what so many of us look forward to after spending several decades toiling away at a 9 to 5 job to bring home a steady paycheck each month. We all have different dreams, different visions of what our golden years would look like. Some may paint a picture of a beautiful vacation home, where they spend their days soaking up the sun, relaxing and just enjoying each day as it comes. Others dream of traveling the world, exploring the different sights and cultures that they never had time for when they were too busy trying to earn a living. There are those whose perfect picture of retirement would be spending quality time with their family and friends while enjoying an occasional game of golf now and then. Would you believe it, there are even people who dream of running their own business because retirement to them is when life is just beginning!

These picture perfect retirement scenarios are the dreams of many Americans. However, not everyone might have been fortunate enough to accumulate the nest egg or stash away that small fortune that is required to live such a lifestyle. Most Americans would probably have accumulated anywhere between $100,000 to $250,000, which is nowhere near enough to live out the next several decades of your life given that there will still be recurring expenses, not to mention healthcare costs and medical bills involved. Those six figures may seem like a lot of money at first glance, but when you think about how long your retirement could last (on average, you're looking at two decades), then that amount is going to be barely scraping the surface for you to get by.

A **GoBanking Rates survey** discovered that while many Americans hoped that the money they would have accumulated by the time they hit retirement could perhaps be enough to afford a nice little vacation home or be enough for them to travel the world, the reality was that a staggering 57% of Americans had *less* than $1,000 collected in their savings account. Even more alarming was the **Stanford Center for Longevity report** which brought to light that almost a third of the baby boomer generation had no money saved in their retirement plans. Given that most experts are advising that we have at least more than $1 million in savings to get us through our retirement years, it looks like most Americans are still a long way off from achieving that financial goal. Even then, experts say that $1 million *might* not be quite enough.

How Long Can $1 Million Last Anyway?
There are a lot of factors which need to be considered during retirement. Longer life expectancies, the rising cost of living, not to mention the rising medical costs. With all the little things that can easily be overlooked, many people don't have a clue as to how much they would need to retire comfortably without having to worry.

Is $1 million enough to retire with?

Dave Ramsey, one of America's most trusted sources when it comes to all things financial advice related, weighs in on this topic on his **website** and points out that for a long time, this was considered the dream retirement financial number. With $1 million in retirement, you could live out your retirement dreams *and* even leave an impressive legacy behind. Now, a million dollars may not be enough to get the job done the way it would have several years ago.

How much you're going to need for your retirement-that magic number that everyone is looking towards-is going to depend *entirely on you.* There is no magic number. The number that you need to see you through is going to depend on the lifestyle you intend to live after you've left your job and the promise of a steady pay for good. If you intend to maintain the same lifestyle you have had all these years, with an expensive house, expensive car, fancy clothes *and* traveling the world at the same time or buy that vacation home you planned for your retirement, then no, $1 million probably isn't going to cut it. However, if you're willing to make adjustments, cut back on several things (but still live a lifestyle where you're happy and comfortable), the number that you're going to need is then going to look very different.

Don't forget that good old Uncle Sam takes his fair share of the cut too, *even* in retirement, especially if your savings is sitting in accounts which are tax-deferred like the IRA or 401K. Any money that is being taken out of those accounts will be subject to income taxes, and that's something you're going to have to take into consideration too. These numbers could end up tripping you up, leaving you shocked or surprised that you ended up with less money that you may have initially anticipated.

Should I Be Worried? Relax! You Can Do This!

It is natural to be concerned about your retirement when it feels like your savings might not be enough. A big concern is what happens when you realize you're quickly running out of money and you've still got a long way ahead of you. How do you spend the rest of your retirement days when it looks like the finances you have might not last you through the next decade? These worrying thoughts can be paralyzing, and as the panic starts to set in, you're not quite sure what to do.

Well, the first thing you need to do is relax, and take a deep breathe because it's not as bad as you may think, as you will soon discover progressing through the next several chapters of this book. Sure, the fear of running out of money is a very serious cause for concern, but you are not without options, and that's the good news. If you plan your expenses wisely, and you're willing to make the necessary lifestyle changes, you would need much less than you initially anticipated to live a comfortable retirement. Naturally, lifestyle adjustments, perhaps even some cutbacks, are to be expected because you can no longer carry on the way you did when you were bringing in a steady paycheck each month. Again, don't worry, because these lifestyle adjustments are not as bad as they sound. Instead of paying for that gym membership each month, for example, scrap that in favor of free activities, like going for a walk in the park or hiking outdoors. Instead of eating out several times a week, scrap that in favor of preparing healthier home cooked meals which are significantly cheaper than dining in a fancy restaurant.

The secret to surviving and being happy in your retirement years is to shift your perspective and embrace this next chapter of your life with an open mind. It's about adapting to the difference in income level and making the necessary changes to fit this new budget. As long as you've still got your basic necessities for the month covered, life can still be pretty good because lucky us, we live in a world today that comes with a lot more options than it did several years ago. Running an online business out of the comfort of your own home was unheard of before the age of the Internet, and today just about anyone can do it, even retirees who still have that burning passion for continuing to do something actively.

Even When You're Retired, It's Easy to Make Money in 2019
Does anyone ever *really* retire these days anyway? In fact, according to the Transamerica Center for Retirement Studies survey, two-thirds of the Baby Boomer generation surveyed claimed that intended to work even after the age of 65, while some planned not to retire at all.

Technology has made a lot of things possible, including opening new doors and opportunities for more ways to earn an income even after retirement. The digital world has opened many pathways, and if you're bold enough to seize the opportunities as they come, anything is possible. Just because you have now hit the retirement milestone, it doesn't mean that your life has slowed down and there's nothing left for you to offer. Not at all! You have *more* to offer than you think you do. All those years spent working hard, all the skills, knowledge and life wisdom that you gained along the way, are valuable! The savvy, entrepreneur minded individual can easily work that to their advantage by turning those skills into an after-retirement side business and additional income stream.

Consultancy businesses, freelancing, tutoring, coaching, creating a new product or service to offer are all opportunities to put all those accumulated skills to good use. We will be exploring more of in the later chapters that talk about specific online business opportunities. The point is, you have valuable life experience to offer, and this can easily turn into an opportunity to earn an income. There is no reason to worry even if you feel like you may not have accumulated enough! There are always options. *Always.*

Be Flexible, Be Open Minded and Anything Is Possible
The key to surviving your financial state even after retirement is to be creative and open-minded because this can lead to a lot more opportunities for you to make money. Instead of worrying about what's going to happen when your money runs out, or whether you've saved up enough, why not switch that around and think about taking a chance instead? If you do want to continue working and keep using all the skills and work experience you have picked up over the years, why not do it? Nothing is holding you back except your own worry. Some employers even now offer the option of shifting to fewer work hours or offering those over the age of 65 more flexible work hours and arrangements, so there is no *necessity* to really "stop" working if you feel like you've got more to contribute. Instead of constantly worrying about it as your retirement age draws near, speak to your employer about what options

11

are available to see if you could work something out, especially if you have been with the company or the organization for several years. If your manager sees you as a valuable contribution to the company, they might be more than happy to try and work something out. Some employees act as contractors after retirement for the services they rendered to their employer before they retired. Even if they say no, at least you know that you tried, rather than just worrying out it without taking any action.

A lot of things are going to change after retirement, including your priorities. The location where you live may not be such a big factor anymore if you don't have to live in a place that is a closer commute to the office or within a good school district. There's no necessity to live in a place that is accessible to public transport anymore if you're not going to be commuting to work so often. Perhaps you don't even need such a big home if your children are all grown up and it's just you and your husband or wife living in a four-bedroom home. As you get older, a single unit or a smaller apartment with no stairs to deal with might start to seem like a better idea, especially for your knees (thinking long-term).

Retirement is about creatively finding a new approach to living that is going to be *right for you* and your current circumstances. This significantly helps lessen the pressure that comes with worrying about your finances if you see that there is no real need to keep up or maintain the lifestyle you had become accustomed to when you were working. Is downsizing such a bad thing if it makes sense to do so? If you can eliminate some of your biggest expenses, suddenly life seems to become a little bit more manageable financially. This may be one appealing option.

Aren't I Too *Old* to Start Making Money Online?
Absolutely not. The only thing that can stop you from making money online is yourself, not your age. It is never too late, especially not with how things change so quickly on the internet. New ways, methods and opportunities are constantly being invented regularly, and if you're brave enough to forgo the excuses and seize the day, nothing can stop you from trying to make money online except self-doubt.

Forget the mentality of constantly trying to race against the clock, because that's a race that is only going to leave you stressed out. That has held you back long enough. How many times in your life have you found yourself wanting to try or do something, but you held back because you thought you were too old to do so? How many times have you felt regret over the missed opportunities that should have been taken? Age is just a number, as cliche as it sounds, and you're only as "old" as you allow yourself to *think* that you are. It isn't just the internet that has changed dramatically, the world as we know it has evolved in drastic ways too. A 50-year old today has a lot more opportunities and can do more things than a 50-year old several decades ago. With the advancements in medicine and the healthier lifestyle changes that we have come to learn of in recent years, many people continue to remain youthful and full of life well into their 70s and 80s!

Instead of using age as a barrier that stops you from living your best life, *embrace* your age because age is accompanied with experience and wisdom. You may not be in your 20s anymore, but see that as a *good thing* because it just means all that life experience can now be put to good use to your advantage. Knowing will give you a significant advantage over the younger generation, especially if you're thinking about starting a business of your own. Have confidence in the fact that you know a lot more things today than you did when you were in your 20s or 30s. Opportunities that you may have been too afraid to ask for when you were younger are now yours to be seized. When you release those insecurities and doubts from your mind, you'll start to see the opportunities with greater clarity.

The *"I'm too old for this"* mentality is a thing of the past. It's a whole new world that we're living in, and as long as you let go of the notion that your "best years are behind you," you'll start to see that there are many possibilities that lie right in front of you. You will see this more and more as you set goals for yourself that encourage you to continue living your life and not slow down. Whenever you find yourself saying *"I wish I could do this, but I'm too old for it now"* stop yourself right there. That is no way to think. What you should be doing is seeing retirement as an opportunity for you to pursue the dreams and goals that you never got a chance to pursue while working. Now that have all the extra time that you need while not working at a job from 9 to 5, what better way to make use of that time than to start putting all your energy into making your dreams a reality? The *"I'm too old for this"* mentality is nothing more than an excuse, and it will only hold you back as long as you allow it to. When you're too busy chasing your dreams and being happy with your life, you don't even think about how old you are anymore.

The best way to get over the hump of feeling old is to surround yourself with other individuals who have not let their retirement years slow them down. Being around other like-minded individuals will provide you with the much needed positive outlook and encouragement! Especially when you see how much these individuals are accomplishing despite their age. It will inspire you to do the same. Be part of an organization or a community of small online business owners for example, share in their wisdom and gain insight into how they got their business off the ground. Research your area of interest and see which other individuals have managed to achieve success and reinvent themselves at a later age.

Not everyone is destined to find their success at a young age in life. Just look at Colonel Sanders, for example. If he had let his age (he was 65 back when he started Kentucky Fried Chicken) stop him from pursuing his dream, we might not be enjoying his fried chicken today. Colonel Sanders never let his rejection from more than 1,000 restaurants or his age slow him down! When no restaurant wanted to buy his recipe, he started his own business. Thanks to him, millions of people all over the world are enjoying his delicious fried chicken recipe, all because he never let his age stop him from going after what he wanted. Peter Mark Roget, who created the Roget's Thesaurus did so at the age of 73, and he did it back in 1852 when all the technology and tools that we have today didn't even exist!

Roget did not let that stop him, neither did he let his age hold him back, and his thesaurus is still being used to this very day. If you think that's impressive, then you'll be blown away to realize that Grandma Moses started her rise to fame at the age of 76. Yes, 76 was when she started finding her passion for paintings, and while she may have only managed to sell them for two to three dollars, over time, her reputation and success grew that one of her famous paintings was sold for 1.2 million dollars in 2016.

Still, think you're too old to achieve success after retirement? Those three inspirational figures certainly didn't, and neither my friend, should you.

Chapter 2: Get an Overview and Become Creative

In Chapter 1, we touched on how $1 million might not be quite enough to get you through retirement, even though that is the most common amount cited to be able to retire comfortably. Just forget this daunting figure! According to **GOBankingRates**, you could easily wipe out that $1 million amount in *12 years! Never mind that very few have been able to save this amount! Instead, we will get creative and create residual passive income, while finding ways to cut expenses!*

Debt is one of the biggest financial burdens of many Americans. Ideally, you'd want to go into your retirement years with no debt at all, but this is not always possible. The **US Government** averages the month Social Security check at $1,404, with more than 40% of adults who are single deriving more than 90% of their monthly income from that Social Security check. The **Government Accountability Office** then points out between 2002 and 2015, more than 500% of those over the age of 65 years who have their Social Security check amounts significantly reduced because of the debts (student loans to be specific) that they need to cover. Another big reason why it's getting harder for older Americans to retire debt free is because of the mortgage payments that they still need to cover.

Getting an overview of your biggest expenses before and after retirement will give you a better idea of where you stand financially. Whether you've saved enough and how long your money is going to last is going to be impacted by the debt that you have. It may be stressful to have this amount staring you in the face when you consolidate all the outstanding debt that you have, but if you want to avoid getting into even *more debt* after you retire, and passing your financial problems onto your family, getting a clear overview of all the outstanding debt and assets that you have is a necessary part of the process.

First, look at your debt, *then* look at the assets that you've got which you might be able to sell to help pay off some of your debt. Make a list of all the outstanding debt that you have and start working on paying them off one by one, especially if you're still working. Your aim should be to pay off as much debt as you possibly can, and you do that by getting creative about what you're going to do after retirement.

To calculate that one number that you would need to retire, many financial advisors and experts are falling back on what is known as the 4% sustainable withdrawal ratio. This is going to essentially be the withdrawal amount that you can take out in both good times and bad, *yet* your financial portfolio can still last you 30 years or more. The 4% formula is the number that is going to help you determine approximately how much you're going to need for your retirement if you need some framework to work around. To figure out this magic number that you would need for your retirement years, simply flip the 4% rule and start working on your calculations from there. Start by dividing your annual spending by 0.04, or multiply that number by 25, and you'll have your target. If you plan to live with

$30,000 annually for example, then based on the 4% rule calculation, your estimated number is going to be approximately $750,000 (which is $30,000 divided by 0.04), and this is the number that you're going to need in your bank annually to retire in a comfortable fashion.

Tony Robbins, the best-selling author of The *Money: Master Game* has a different approach to figuring out how much you would need for retirement. His two-step approach involves figuring out how much money it is going to take for you to maintain the lifestyle that you want (how much you're spending), and then multiply that number by 20. The bottom line, though, is that there *is no "magic number"* that is going to set you up for a life where you never have to worry again. Things change, situations and circumstances change, and it comes down to the more money you have saved, and the more passive income you can create, the more security you will have in your retirement years.

There's no better time to get creative than during your retirement years (or the years leading up to your retirement). When you start giving some serious thought about the options that you could start looking into, you avoid staring into that foreboding financial abyss where no steady income, no job, and inadequate savings stares right back at you. Not everyone is fortunate enough to have a substantial nest egg, or a trust fund of cash stashed away for, so for the rest of us, the only thing that is left to do is to start planning and get creative. Even if you don't have enough money tucked away by the time you collect your last drawn salary, don't worry because there are still ways to remedy the situation, as we're about to explore in this chapter.

Picture Perfect - Visualizing Your Perfect Retirement Day

Endless sunny days spent soaking up the sunshine as you gaze out at the crystal blue sea waters from your beachfront vacation home. Spending the rest of your days traveling the world, exploring country after country as you immerse yourself in the delightful experience of seeing somewhere new. Lively music coming from the deck of your cruise ship that was sailing across the ocean towards the next port. The laughter of family and loved ones gathered around your home as you spend quality time together.

At some point , you would have pictured what life in your retirement would look like, and how you hoped to live out the remainder of your days. If you haven't already retired yet, then visualizing your perfect retirement life is a good way to get started. Why? Because it gives you an idea of what you hope to achieve. This gives you clear goals to work towards instead of having just a vague picture of "if's" and "maybe's." Being able to visualize the details of your perfect retirement life is how you *know* for sure what you want, your desires, your hopes and your dreams for what life could be like once you've stopped the daily grind of working Mondays to Fridays in the same routine.

The act of visualization is more than just being able to paint a pretty picture in your mind that brings a smile to your face. It's about connecting your present self now to the person in that not too distant future, which will then lead you to start thinking about how and what you can do to make that vision come true. By *knowing* what you want in the future, you can start thinking about the action steps which need to be taken right now to get you one step closer. The more details you can put into this visualized image, the better you'll be able to think about how you're going to make it happen. For example, if you were to picture yourself flying off to Thailand as your first location a week after you retire, visualize yourself packing, how long you'll be gone for, how much the flight tickets are going to cost, what hotel you're going to be staying at, where you intend to tour once you land in the country, how you plan to spend your time and more. Visualizing all of this will lead you to then plan and prepare by doing as much research as possible about Thailand, look up how much the flight tickets and hotels are going to possibly cost, what your average daily spending could look like and how long you could afford to live there, what places there are to visit, the activities that you want to do and so on. You see how this is already much better than simply saying I'm going to visit Thailand and having no clue about where to stay, what to do, or how much it's going to cost?

Even better, think about creating a vision board of your dream retirement life and put it somewhere in your home where you could look at it every day to serve as a reminder to yourself of what you're working towards. A vision board should be a collection of everything that motivates and inspires you to keep on going, and you'll know you have created the perfect vision board when you feel moved to take some action each time that you look at it.

Life doesn't have to slow once when you retire. There are plenty of options to keep that money rolling that could help *support* the lifestyle you envision for yourself. Which means that even if you don't have quite enough saved at this point in life to support your ideal retirement lifestyle, it could still be within your grasp if you play your cards right.

Let's Start With Finding Your Unique Talents and Passion

Have you got a special talent? Or a hobby or interest that you are extremely passionate about? What special skills do you have that could be put to good use? What is your calling in life? What do you feel that you were always meant to do? These are questions that we all ponder at some stage during our life, regardless of how old we may be and whether we're retired or not. Working a steady job can take up a substantial portion of your time, especially when you've got other responsibilities to juggle like having a family to look after or other commitments that need your attention.

Perhaps you've had almost little to no time to pursue these areas of interest seriously in the past, but now that you're retired, the opportunity has arisen for you to start giving it some serious consideration. In fact, this interest or hobbies of yours just might help you create that dream retirement life you want. It's time to break out those hidden skills and talents that you possess, and if you're not quite sure how to discover what you're good at, here's a good place to start:

Step #1: *Think About Your Dreams*
What have you always wished you could do? What have

you dreamed of doing as a child or an adult? If you were given the opportunity to live your dream life, your *ideal life*, what would you be doing? We all have dreams and those secret hidden desires of what we would like to be or do, dreams which may have been forgotten along the way as life took over. Now you have the time to start thinking about them again! Write them down, so you have a list to start working with. Brainstorm! The sky is the limit!

Step #2: Talking to Family and Friends

Now that you've got a list prepared of what you would love to do or what you're passionate about, start talking to family and friends and see what *they* think you're good at. They might even point out something that they think you do well, but it never occurred to you to see that as one of your talents. This step is one of the easiest ways to discover what some of your strengths may be, especially because you can trust the source that it is coming from. Family and your closest friends are there to give you their honest opinion because they want you to succeed. They want to see you thrive and they'll be more than happy to be candid about they think you may -or may not- be great at. Family and friends are also the targeted audiences because these are the people who have been around you the longest, who know you well enough to give some insight. It'll be interesting to hear their perspective, because they may point out something you may not have realized and that could spark a lightbulb moment where you think, *"You know what? That's actually not a bad idea!"*.

Step #3: Think About Your Life Experiences

Next, think about all your life experiences so far and how

that can be tied into what you think you want to pursue. If you've traveled abroad extensively for work, how might that help if you're thinking about starting an online business selling products? If you spent years in the education sector, how might that help now as you think about branching out your passion for teaching into an online business of some sort? What could you offer? How could you turn these skills and experiences into a marketable business or service that other people would be willing to pay for? The home education market is booming. Online platforms such as Pinterest particularly cater to many parents looking for educational activities. Tutoring is in high demand! This can be done online in todays world many times.

Offering your unique talents and sharing your passion with the rest of the world is a great launchpad for something better, which is this case would be turning into a business that you love. There's an old saying that goes "Do what you love, and you'll never have to work a day in your life." (Author unknown) Do what you love during your retirement years, and it won't feel like you're working at all.

What Are Your Goals for Retirement?
Carl Jung once said that your vision would only start to become clearer when you start looking into your own heart. When you look into your heart about what vision you see for yourself when you retire, what does your heart show you? Ask several retirees about what they see themselves doing, and the most common answer that is likely to pop up would have something to do with traveling. While that

vision may be great, there is a much bigger question which needs to be addressed. *How do we turn that vision into a reality?* That's where retirement goals come into play.

Step #1: Start Planning

The first step of any goal-setting process is to start planning, planning, planning. Write it down ! Make a detailed list about what your dream retirement life looks like. Leave no detail out, no matter how small it may be. Write it all down so you can have a very clear picture of *what* you want to accomplish. This then makes the *how* to accomplish part much easier. Questions that you need to think about as you begin mapping out what your dream retirement life include the following: What is the overall vision that you see in your mind? What's on the to-do list? What are you most excited about? What would you like to accomplish during this time? Last but not least, What would you miss the most about your working life? (the kind of work you would miss the most)?

Step #2: Start Writing Down the Specifics

Moving onto to step number two, which is where you will begin setting very specific goals for yourself based on the details of the vision you mapped out in Step 1. If your goal was to visit five countries within the first year of retirement, *how* would you accomplish that? If your goal was to turn your hobby into a profitable online business within 3 years of retiring, *what* would you need to do to start working towards that goal? Separating your goals and breaking them down into several categories will better help you with the specifics. Separate your goals into:

- Short-term goals and long-term goals
- Needs and wants

This will help you prioritize your goals in the order of which they should be worked on.

Step #3: Always Ask Yourself What Do You Want

With every goal that you set, you need to ask yourself one very important question. *What do you want?* When you've got your response, write it down next to your goal. Repeat the same exercise for each goal that you've written down earlier, so you know exactly why you're doing this and what outcome you hope to achieve at the end of it.

Step #4: Think About the Costs

Now that you've got your goals in place, the next step that you need to think about is how much it is going to cost you to achieve that goal. This is the financial planning aspect of the process, and here is where you start mapping out the financial steps that are going to turn that goal into a reality. Go back to the example where your goal was to travel to at least five different countries within the first year of your retirement. How much would that cost you and what finances would need to be readjusted to make that work? Is your current cash portfolio able to support this goal and if not, what could be done to make it happen?

Step #5: Choose Your Priorities

Here is where separating your goals into short-term, long-term, needs, and wants comes in handy. It lets you prioritize which goal you should be working towards achieving first without causing you to lose sight of all your other goals. When you're retired, you feel like the world is your oyster. You want to do anything, and everything and you feel like you want to do it *right this minute*. While we would all love to do that, unfortunately, unless you're rolling in cash, you're going to need to take a step back, set some goals and realistic look at which goal takes priority and start working towards making that happen first before working on everything else.

What To Do When You're Hit With Unexpected Bills
Even when you're working a steady job, and unexpected bills hit, you're going to feel the financial pinch of it. What more when you retire with *no* steady paycheck to fall back on. There are some expenses which can't be helped at times. An unexpected home repair. An unexpected car repair. A health problem that needs to be dealt with. These unexpected bills and expenses can come out of nowhere and hit you hard when you're not quite prepared for it, which is why as the Northwestern Mutual Planning & Progress Study points out, 55% of Americans are worried about what to do when they find themselves face to face with a financial emergency they simply don't have enough funds for.

Depending on what you're dealing with, these emergencies could set your retirement plans back substantially. Needless to say, of course, it is always best to start preparing straight away while you can, *before* that financial emergency comes at you hard. If you're about to retire soon, start making preparations now, and if you're already retired, it is never too late to start taking some action right this minute.

• **Get Yourself an Emergency Fund ASAP** - Ideally, you'll want to have at least $1,000 in an emergency fund stashed away in an easy to access account. If you haven't retired just yet, start tucking away any spare cash you can find and once you have accumulated at least $1,000, put it into a bank account, and that's your emergency fund. If you're already retired and you've got $1,000 to spare, open another bank account and keep your emergency fund there. If you don't, start putting funds aside little by little from your monthly budget until you have accumulated that amount. It is recommended that you keep this emergency funds in a *separate* account to all your other funds because you don't want to risk accidentally using it all up and suddenly finding yourself stuck with no money. This is why you kept your savings in a separate account, and now you need to do the same for your emergency fund. Instead of putting money aside for retirement, you're putting aside money for an emergency. As you go along, continuously top up that emergency fund and let the money accumulate until such time when an actual emergency arises. You'll be glad that you did. It will also provide some peace of mind in pursing your dreams.

• **Make Some Cut Backs to Your Budget** - Take a good look at what your current budget is like right now. Is there anything that is unnecessary that you could survive without? If there is, cut out those expenses and put that money instead towards your emergency fund. Activities such as going to the movies once a week, or dining out several times a week could be scaled back on for the next few months, and those funds diverted instead towards preparing an emergency nest egg for yourself.

- **Any Assets You No Longer Require?** - Have you got any big-ticket items or assets in your home that you no longer need? You might want to think about selling those off and putting the cash that you get from that towards your emergency fund instead. If you and your spouse no longer have a need for two cars now that you're both retired, consider selling one of them off and putting the cash towards helping you prepare for an emergency instead.

Leaving a Lasting Legacy Behind

As we start to get older, we begin to really think about the legacy that we are going to leave behind, especially for our children. You don't need to be a multimillionaire to leave behind a legacy that your family will remember you for because what matters more than a financial is leaving behind a legacy of character and wisdom that reminds them of all you taught them. Don't worry too much about leaving behind a substantial sum of money for your children. Instead, think about the life lessons and the wisdom that you could leave them with, priceless memories that money cannot buy. Whether you leave them with a small sum or a large amount, it's the kind of person you will be remembered as at the end of the day that truly matters.

If you do want to leave your family with some form of finances even if you think you may not have saved enough, there are still ways in which you could achieve that.

• **Getting Life Insurance -** It might not seem to make sense to purchase life insurance once you've retired, but you're now doing this for your family more so than yourself. A life insurance policy that leaves your family with some form of financial benefit once you're no longer around could be a big help because they could then use those funds (if needed) to help pay for the taxes on your estate, cover any other family debts or costs which might have been incurred (medical or funeral costs), providing them some extra funds to put into paying off their college debt or even putting those into their own savings account. It is wise to consult an agent with experience for your age group.

• **Leaving Your Assets to Them -** If you own your home or a family vacation home of some sort, pass it on to your loved ones as part of the legacy that you leave behind. Even if they have homes of their own, they could choose to live it in, renovate your home and then sell it, or perhaps even rent it out for some extra income.

• **Leaving Behind Your Business -** Another reason to consider starting an online business in your retirement years is that this business can continue and it is something for you to leave behind for your family as part of your legacy. More importantly, you leave them with the knowledge that anything is possible even after retirement, especially starting a thriving business.

• **Leaving Your 401K -** If you anticipate having some retirement money leftover, designate who your beneficiaries will be with your 401K account. You might need to check with the HR department of your company if you're still working about how your account is structured and what steps would need to be taken to make that happen. Be sure to discuss with your accountant the specifics.

• **Leaving Behind Your IRA -** If you have an Individual Retirement Account (IRA) and anticipate having some money left over, name your family members as your beneficiaries to which the account will be transferred. If you have several members of your family with whom you would like to leave a little something, then divide the accounts up equally for each family member and designate a specified amount that each person is going to receive. Roth IRA accounts are a good bet since these accounts are not taxed when you start making withdrawals from them and you can designate multiple family members as beneficiaries to this account.

Chapter 3: Your Perfect Business

Go to school. Graduate. Go to college. Get a degree. Get a good, steady paying job. Work for several years. Retire. That was the norm, and for a long time, that was how it was. You worked, and then you retired. Generations before us survived this way, and they made it work. Perhaps the finances at that time were much better suited to those conditions too. Houses were not as expensive as they are today, and the cost of living was significantly more affordable. The world that we are living in today, however, is a very different scenario. Retirement no longer means just kicking up your heels and relaxing the rest of your life away (unless you want to of course). Retirement these days could be the start of a brand-new beginning, and it's high time we did away with the old ideas and make room for a world of new possibilities.

Turning Your Passion into Profession
If there's something that you're passionate about and you've always wanted to pursue, but never had the time to do so because of work and other commitments that might have got in the way, well guess what? You don't have to contend with your job any more now that you're retired. The time has come to pursue your passion! There's no better time to start doing what you love than right now, especially if you're concerned about keeping an income coming in. The most successful businesses out there are the ones which have been built on passion, not the ones that have been just started for the sake of money. While it is true that money and earning potential is among the many

reasons to venture into the business world, without passion, you're going to be hard-pressed to keep on going when challenges start to hit you left and right. Believe me; there will most definitely be challenges because make no mistake, running a business is not easy. That's why you've got to do something you *love*, something that makes you want to get out of bed each day with gusto and enthusiasm because you can't wait to get to work on your business.

Pursing a passion helps to overcome the obstacles that will happen, pushing you out of your comfort zone! It is your passion and your love for what you do that keep you moving forward. It is your passion that strengthens your resolve to never give up. If you were running a business just for the sake of money, it wouldn't be long before you start to question if this is worth your time and energy. In those seasons that always come and go, when things start to become difficult, quitting starts to look like an appealing option, it is your passion for what you do and why you want to do it that keeps you steady!

Besides passion, there are several other factors that need to be taken into consideration when attempting to build the perfect business for yourself. Several areas to consider are:

- **What Are Your Strengths?** - Think back to the job you've had for the past several decades. What skills or talents have you developed over that period that you have been repeatedly commended for? Your leadership skills maybe? Perhaps it was how you had a knack with people and a real gift for sales. Maybe it was your copywriting abilities. Or the creative spark in you

33

that help developed hundreds of fantastic advertisements and logo designs for your company. How do those strengths then tie in with your passion, and how can you get them to work together? Everyone is good at something in their jobs; it is now time to look at tapping into your existing strengths and using them as leverage to pursuing your passion.

• **What's Your Vision? -** Go back to the visualization exercise for a bit. When you think about having a business of your own, what kind of vision do you see? Paint a detailed picture and think about the necessary steps that need to be taken towards making it happen. If cooking is your passion and you're thinking about forming your own catering company after you retire, what sort of vision do you see for yourself and your business? What does your clientele look like? The kind of food you serve? What would you need to do to turn that passion into a profession?

• **Are You Rushing into It?** - If you're one of the lucky people who already know what your passion and your talents are good for you! As eager as you may be to hit the ground running and get your business going as soon as you hit retirement, take a step back for a minute and ask yourself if you're rushing things? You may know what your passion is and what your strengths are, but do you know what it takes to run a business? Passion alone is not going to cut it without the business know-how, and it is imperative that you look before you leap, especially with something as life-changing as starting a business of your own. Do your due diligence, get as much perspective as possible by talking to others who may be in a similar field, assess all the risks involved before making some calculated risks of your own.

• **Have You Joined A Relevant Community Online?** - There's a group or online community for just about anything these days, especially for retirees looking to start some sort of business on the side after they've left their full-time jobs. The best way to familiarize yourself with the industry and market demands of the area you're thinking about getting into is to join an online community for an insiders perspective. It will help you keep your expectations realistic also, so that you don't end up getting discouraged if something doesn't work out as you hoped. Reach out to the online community, ask questions, make connections, and build a rapport with the people that you connect with. You never know, these connections could be useful down the road when you've got your business up and running.

Welcome to the World of Freelancing
If running a full-fledged business is not exactly what you're looking for, once again, technology has come to the rescue by providing us with other avenues to choose. Isn't it great that we live in an age where options are almost

everywhere around us? If one pathway isn't the ideal choice, there's always something else to fall back on. If the entrepreneurship destiny is not one that you think belongs to you, welcome to the world of freelancing.

Freelancing is often associated with creative jobs, especially writing, editing, proofreading, marketing, or graphic designing. These areas alone hold plenty of opportunities for those who love setting their own work hours and working at their own pace. You are free to choose to work full-time or part-time. However, freelancing has now branched out into other new avenues also! Transcription, data entry, virtual assistant jobs, online tutoring, blogger, photographer, author, computer graphics illustrator, Etsy shop owner, the possibilities are literally endless. If you've got a skill, talent, or passion, you could easily market those skills and turn it into a freelance business of your own.

These freelance job avenues offer anyone with a computer, good internet connection, and the required skills the ability to make extra money in their own time. You can also enroll in online courses or community college classes if you want to take your skills to the next level. Becoming a full-time or part-time freelancer is a business of its own. You're now working for yourself. It is up to you to network with your clients, forge lasting connections that will make them returning customers, deliver a fantastic finished product as promised, and pocket the profit that you receive.

What happens if you're someone who is not exactly tech savvy though, and you can barely bring yourself to switch on a computer without cringing and hoping that nothing goes wrong? Well, you'll be happy to know that freelancing isn't just limited to the online world alone (options are such a wonderful thing !). Tap into your passion, strengths, and skills and market yourself as a freelancer for other jobs that don't require you to be a tech-savvy expert. Event planning, wedding coordinating, a casual hours childcare worker, pet care services, property manager, even selling arts and crafts, for example, are all examples of freelance businesses that you could start without ever having to rely a hundred percent on a computer. In choosing a business, it all comes down to what you love to do, what you're good at, and what services or products you would like to offer and how flexible you want to be! Check with your local library or community centers for courses on computer skills for help also.

How Would I Market Myself as A Freelancer?

The easiest and cheapest way to do so would be through online channels. Three specifically, which are Facebook, Fiverr, and Instagram. These three platforms are not just your golden ticket to marketing yourself as a capable and qualified freelancer for hire, but it could also help you source for clients, secure jobs and create an even wider exposure for your business because of the vast reach that this platform has.

Marketing Yourself on Facebook

Facebook is a fantastic social media platform that is great not just for keeping in touch with family and friends, but for building a business too. As the world's leading social media platform with billions of users to its name, the potential exposure that you could get on Facebook surpasses any other social media platform out there.

With more than one billion active daily users on this platform, Facebook is the platform that every freelancer looking to secure new jobs and clients should be active with. With the right methods and strategies, especially with the ample tools that this platform provides through its Facebook Pages, you'll be able to hone in and reach exactly the kind of audience with whom your message is going to resonate the loudest. Facebook Pages are one of the many tools Facebook has made available to both small and big business owners, and it comes equipped with all the right targeting tools that you need to customize your message and choose the kind of audience that you want to reach. Freelancers stand to benefit from this! To get started, you would simply need to, first of all, create a professional looking Facebook page for your freelance business.

The Facebook page that you create for your freelance business *must* be kept separate from your personal profile. You will be marketing yourself as a professional, and all the content that is on your page should only be related to your business. No personal photographs, no personal status updates, nothing that is going to take away the air of professionalism from that page. Your clients need to know who you are, especially when you're just starting out your business and they will want to know as much information as possible about you. When creating your Facebook page, you should aim to fill out every section with as much detail as possible so your clients can really get a firm grasp about what your business offers and why they should consider taking up your services. Highlight your strengths, background, experience, and most importantly, don't forget to include your contact information.

To attract new clients in the hopes of securing more paid work, you need first of all to know who your audience is. You need to identify crucial information such as what age group they fall into, what their interests are, where they are located, what sort of business or services are they looking for, and any other important information which can be gathered about their demographics to help you piece together a specific profile about your clients. When you know who your audience is, you'll then know exactly *how* to tailor your messages to them and speak to them in a way that resonates and makes them take notice of what you are offering. A great tip to remember is to think about the kind of content on your own Facebook newsfeed, which tends to grab your attention the most. What would those be? Photos and video, of course, which is why many businesses boost their products on this platform through these two channels. In fact, if you were to post for photo and video content, your page is **104%** more likely to get a boost in comments, with a **53%** opportunity for more likes. With stats like these, photos and videos are exactly what you should be leveraging on to drive clients to your page.

Marketing Yourself on Instagram
To grow your business, its best chance requires that you make full use of social media platforms. Facebook, being the biggest and most widely used social media platform, is one of them. The other is Instagram. While there are other

social media platforms, work with just two, to begin with, you don't need to be on every single platform out there, especially if it isn't suitable for your business. Besides, you don't want to run the risk of spreading yourself too thin either, so it is best just to pick two platforms and work on perfecting your marketing efforts on those first.

Instagram's popularity is second to Facebook, but if you're going to be using this platform to broaden your search for new clients, you need first to determine if the clients you're targeting are in fact heavy users of this platform. If they aren't, then focusing your efforts on Instagram might not be the best idea since they would be better directed towards a platform that your clients are frequently using instead.

To improve your chances of scoring new clients through Instagram, here's what you need to keep in mind:

- **It's Not About Quantity, It's About Quality -** All too often people get caught up in the number of followers that they have. 200 followers may not seem like a lot, but if they are *authentic* followers who are very engaged with the content you provide, those 200 followers are a lot better than having 500 followers who don't engage with your content at all.

- **Avoid Buying Followers -** Avoid the temptation to buy your followers, for the obvious reason of authenticity. If your followers are not engaging with your content, you won't be getting new business anyway, and fake followers are unlikely to ever engage with your content.

• **Make Your Feed Cohesive -** It's all about quality on Instagram, especially with the content that you post. Unlike Facebook, Instagram relies heavily on visuals and less on captions. Every image that you post has to tell a story, and your content needs to be consistent with the theme of the business and service that you're providing. Try to maintain a similar color scheme for example throughout your feed, of it you're going to be using filters, try to use the same filter for all your images to feel up with the cohesive feel to it.

• **Using Relevant Hashtags -** Instagram is all about the hashtags. A hashtag is a keyword with the number sign used before it. They are used when people search for different topics. If you're trying to market your business on this platform, don't overlook hashtags because they are your best friend. Without them, it makes it significantly harder for your post to show up in relevant search results, let alone at the top of the page. Use hashtags which are relevant to your business. A quick search of the relevant keywords which clients generally use to locate businesses or services just like yours will give you an idea of the kind of hashtags you should be using too. A great tip to keep your profile and your content looking neat and tidy is to put those hashtags in your comments. Hashtags will also come in handy in helping you locate new customers that you could reach out to. Simply key in the hashtag in the search bar of the app, and you'll be able to browse through a list of people and assess which may be interested in your services based on the hashtag that they use and how they use is (is it attached to a question searching for a service for example).

•   **Engage in Comments and Respond to DMs -** A DM on Instagram is referring to Direct Messages. Some clients may prefer to use the DM approach to reach out to you, and you should always respond to your DMs as soon as possible, even if they are just general inquiries about your business. Engage with your followers! If someone leaves a comment or tags you in a post, respond to them. Leave a positive response which leaves them feeling good and, where appropriate, direct them back to your profile or subtly highlight the services that you offer.

•   **Post At Least Once Daily -** Aim to post content at least once a day, so your audience knows that your profile is active and up to date.

Marketing Yourself with Fiverr

Since it was created, Fiverr has grown to become the biggest freelance services platform for digital-based services, especially. Competition with this platform, however, is high, and your profile could go for months without getting a single request. Freelance services on Fiverr are known as 'gigs,' and starting at just $5 per gig, there are hundreds of thousands of new gigs being added to the platform daily. When a client goes onto the website and searches for a particular freelance service, if your profile isn't among the first top search results that turn up, your visibility starts to decrease. Therefore you must find ways to been seen!

Increasing your visibility is going to boil down how you attract new clients. Fiverr works on an algorithm principle just like Google, and if you want your profile to appear at the top of the search results, you're going to have to follow the strategies to boost the visibility of your page. Here is an overview:

• **Make Your Profile Look Professional -** High quality, clear profile pictures are a must if you want clients to sit up and take notice of you. Ideally, you want to try and get a profile picture which represents you within a work environment type of setting. Home office setups would work well too. This creates authenticity and looks professional at the same time.

• **Make Use of Your Description Box -** If you're given 1,200 characters to fill up in your description box, use up every single one of it. The more details you can include about yourself and the services you provide, the better. Avoid being vague and sketchy. When you're writing up the profile, put yourself in your client's perspective, and ask yourself if you would you be impressed by what you read? Would you hire yourself? Details matter, especially when it comes to highlighting your strengths. Ask yourself why your clients should choose you over every other profile on Fiverr.

• **Get to Know Fiverr -** One of the worst mistakes any entrepreneur (freelancers included) can do is to assume that they know what the client wants. Where instead of listening to the client, you're trying to make predictions and offer services based on what *you think* they want. That is entirely the wrong way to go about it and can cause new freelancers to end up losing customers instead. Instead of predicting, try getting to know your customers by immersing yourself into Fiverr as much as possible. Get to know what the culture is all about by visiting numerous blogs, taking part in social media discussions about them, even reading several books which focus specifically on Fiverr and how it works.

• **Know the Terms and Conditions -** It is highly recommended that you familiarize yourself with the platform's Terms and Conditions and understand exactly how the site works best for sellers such as yourself. Starting off at $5 priced gigs may not seem like much, but you need to work your way to the top and earn the right to increase your prices, just like at work where you've got to earn your way to a higher salary. Just jumping into the water and trying it out is a good way to learn. Hire someone on Fiverr to create an ad, write a promotion, design a poster, or format something you have written. You will learn how to manage the website by doing!

• **Learning to Say No** - Some people struggle with the idea of saying 'no' to their clients because they don't want to run the risk of losing a sale. But when you're in business, that is one of the smartest decisions you could make because it signals that you know what you're worth. There are some clients who can be unreasonably demanding, insisting on outrageous discounts and generally make themselves difficult to work with. Set the standard of working with only professional clients and avoid stressing yourself out unnecessarily by learning how to say 'no' when there is a need for it. You'll attract better clientele this way over time.

• **Making Use of Keyword Modifiers** - A great way to boost your chances of getting picked up by Fiverr's algorithm is to name your gigs using the right kind of keywords. Especially when those keywords are more specific and targeted. For example, instead of just naming your gig 'Freelance Writing Services", add an extra something special to your title like "Freelance Writing Services 24 Hours" to set yourself apart from all the other similarly named freelance writing gigs.

Need to Improve Your Skills? Try Teachable and Udemy

Whenever you feel like your skills need some brushing up on to provide your clients with even better services, online training platforms like Teachable and Udemy are perfect for improving your knowledge about a wide variety of subjects.

Teachable is an online platform known as a Learning Management System (LMS), and you can enroll in a variety of subjects by performing a quick search on their site for the kind of course you're looking for. It is an easy to use platform which is focused on helping entrepreneurs just like you build your brand, and it comes with flexible pricing options too to suit every type of budget. There are even some courses which are offered for free! If you're lucky enough, your course won't end up costing you a single cent.

Udemy is also an LMS which works in a similar fashion but is targeted towards professional adults more so than entrepreneurs. Udemy's course offerings also come in various price points, so you should have no problems finding the right course that is within your budget. As of 2018, the platform has approximately 100,000 courses and more on its platform.

The best part about both these platforms? They provide you with the option of *creating a course* of your own which you could upload on their site. If you've got the skills and expertise to share, creating a course might just be another avenue for you to create a profitable business of your own.

Next we will delve into an overview of several online businesses as examples.

Chapter 4: What Is an Online Business?

Alright, so let's say that you have decided that you want to start an online business that doesn't involve freelancing or marketing a service that you're offering. Are there any other pathways which you could explore? As a matter of fact, there are, and two of the easiest online businesses out there that you could get started on as you start to dip your toes into the online business world are Kindle Direct Publishing and dropshipping.

What's Kindle Direct Publishing?

Amazon isn't just known as the world's largest marketplace! Amazon has developed several other services to add to its impressive portfolio. One of these is its self-publishing tool known as Kindle Direct Publishing (KDP). If you've always wanted to have a book published in your name and become the author you always aspired to be, KDP is the easiest online business model for beginners where anyone - literally *anyone* - can publish a book themselves. No matter what your background may be, where you come from, or what you do, you can become a self-published author and start generating passive income if you've got something of quality to sell. You can even hire contractors on Fiverr to help with the creation of your title!

Believe it or not, people still like to read. It may come as a surprise, given that we seem to be a generation that is hooked on social media and constantly glued to your devices, but the great thing about KDP is that it is *accessible on a device.* The eBook marketplace especially has grown in recent years and continues to grow as more people start to realize that publishing a book now has become easier than ever, even if you don't have the technical skills or specialist know-how to get it done.

KDP is the perfect choice as your entry point to the online business world, and there's no better platform to go with than Amazon, which commands an impressive 80% share of the eBook market. Another advantage of choosing KDP is that Amazon is offering the authors anywhere between 35% to 75% royalty on the net revenues that they derive. In comparison, traditional book publishers may only offer between 15% and 20% royalty. For many, KDP is the clear choice!

When you publish your book on KDP, you're publishing for life. Your book will be there forever as long as you want it to be (could be a nice little legacy to leave behind also). The best part of this entire process is that Amazon themselves will help you promote your book! If you were worried about how to market your content, Amazon is here once more to provide the solution.

All you need is a great idea (or several) or a book, and you're ready to get started on your journey towards becoming the next published author on Amazon.

Why Should I Choose KDP ?
True, there are many other self-publishing platforms available to choose from. Barnes & Noble Press, Lulu, Author House, or Book Baby are just some of the many other platforms some authors have chosen to go with. Every platform comes with their own strengths and

weaknesses, and three of the main reasons why you KDP might just be the best choice for you include:

•   You get to keep control of the rights to your book and set your own prices within their guidelines.
•   You can make changes to your book whenever you feel like it.
•   KDP takes a very small royalty percentage compared to other platforms.
•   Most eBooks and print books which get published via KDP come with worldwide distribution rights.

How Exactly Do I Make *Money* with KDP?
You've got four options to choose from when it comes to making money through this self-published author avenue. These four choices that you're presented with are Kindle books, paperback and hardcover books, and audio books. Kindle books are the easiest to get started with for self-published authors.

There's still a big demand for paperback books too, especially when it comes to books for children since parents generally prefer having a physical copy of the book for their child to explore using their senses. Paperback books are among the few products which are considered evergreen, and you can certainly capitalize on this aspect. Choosing to publish paperback books is a simple process that can be learned. It only takes a few minutes to set up your book on Amazon when you've got the file ready on hand. Paperbacks sell at higher price points, which means you could earn more royalties than with an ebook.

Hardcover books are slightly more challenging that paperback because of the higher price point. This may cause some readers to hesitate since they could get the same copy in a much cheaper paperback version. But your product could still appeal to those who love collecting hardcover books, so why not have an additional revenue stream to cater to those who love holding a hard copy of what they are reading? You will have to use a third party to get your hardcover book published since at this time KDP doesn't produce hardcover content. **Lulu** would be a good third party platform to consider and there are others you will find as you research.

Last but not least, audiobooks are quickly and easily created through yet another Amazon sister company, **Audiobook Creation Exchange** (ACX). It is essentially the same version of your book, except in audio format to create another income stream. All that is needed from you is to hire a narrator to produce your book on ACX and you're good to go. Your books will then be sold via Audible and promoted by Amazon itself.

KDP vs. KDP Select
Wait, there are two versions of the KDP? There certainly is, and you'll have to decide on which option you're going to go with before you begin selling your content on Amazon. Should you choose to with KDP, you'll be choosing the non-exclusive option, which means that you can have the choice of selling your books to other eBook retailers too. You won't be exclusively tied to Amazon Kindle alone.

With the KDP Select option, on the other hand, you'll be giving Amazon exclusive distribution rights to all the books you produce on Kindle. You won't be able to sell your content to other eBook retailers like Google Play, Nook, or Apple. The rights will be exclusive to KDP alone until that exclusivity period draws to an end.

Next we will explore another popular online business idea. Droppshipping!

Dropshipping Explained
You've probably come across the term dropshipping before, but you're not quite sure what it is and how it works. In a nutshell, dropshipping is a retail fulfillment process, *except* that the merchant who is selling that product does not actually keep the item in stock. The item is instead shipped to the customer by a third party supplier when the order is placed. This means that the shop owner (the merchant) does not physically handle the product themselves. They may not even see the product at all. Dropshipping apart from the other online retail business models by the fact that you (the merchant) does physically own any of the stock or inventory Instead, the merchant contracts a third party supplier who will ship the products directly to the customer once they receive the order details. The customer still places their orders through the merchants online store, but the third party supplier is the one who ships the product to them.

There are four main reasons to consider dropshipping when starting a new business online.

• **Reason 1: You Don't Need as Much Capital.** Setting up a business is not easy, especially your average brick and mortar establishment. Getting a business going can cost you well into the thousands, perhaps even six figures! Not so with Dropshipping! Dropshipping provides the ideal solution because one of the greatest benefits is the fact that it isn't necessary to invest a lot of capital. You don't have to purchase any products, you don't have to fork out major upfront cash for inventory investments, and you won't have to deal with various other bills like utilities, overhead costs, employee salary and more because everything is done online.

• **Reason 2: It Is the Easiest E-commerce Business to Start.** Life becomes significantly simpler when you don't have to deal with many of the other aspects of running a business such as paying for a warehouse, tracking your inventory accounts, packing your orders, shipping your orders, handling the return of your orders, and constantly ordering products to maintain your stock levels! These are not going to be a problem at all for you because the third-party supplier will handle all of these aspects!

• **Reason 3: The Very, Very Low Cost of Overhead.** With so many costs taken out of the picture, dropshipping is going to cost you as little as $100 per month to run your business. All you require is your laptop and a good internet connection.

- **Reason 4: Dabble in A Wide Product Selection.** Since you have the advantage of not having to pre-order your stock, dropshipping presents you with another benefit of being able to offer a large selection of products. This broadens your customer base and increases your potential for sales. If you have suppliers to work with, you can offer as many products as you'd like on your website.

Of course, just like every other business model, drop shipping does have its drawbacks. One is being the low-profit margins that you stand to make. Drop shipping has grown to become a very competitive niche market because of the fact that it is a low investment startup. You're going to have to compete against hundreds of other merchants selling the same product, many of which are willing to sell at very low prices and minuscule profit margins in an attempt to grow their business. There could also be inventory issues to contend with, as sometimes your supplier might run out of stock and could be unable to fulfill your order. Since your customers will only have you as the point of contact, it will be your responsibility to handle any queries or unpleasant service reports that you receive from them. Shipping complexities are something to be considered also since you will be working with many suppliers. Doing the research and reading reviews can help you choose your suppliers wisely.

How the Dropshipping Order Process Works
Here's how the dropshipping process works. It first starts with you, the merchant. You will set up a website, list the

products for sale and their prices, and wait for customers to put in order for the products that they want. Once your customer's order has been confirmed, an email should be sent out to them confirming the details of their order.

Once done, you would then gather their shipping and contact information and proceed to contact your representative at your wholesaler and place an order with the supplier, together with the shipping information from your customer. If the item is in stock, the wholesaler will then proceed to pack the order and ship it out as soon as possible to the address provided by the customer. Once the package has been shipped, the tracking information will be sent to the customer.

When the customer receives the package; however, the contact details on the label will be yours, *not your wholesaler.* This is because you are the point of contact, and your customer knows only your business name as the company with which they have placed their order. The wholesaler in this process will continue to remain anonymous.

Where to Go for More Information
Should you want to learn more about KDP or drop shipping, there are courses available on both Teachable and Udemy where you could explore both these topics in greater depth. Our goal is to provide you with a basic overview of options to give you a general knowledge base some of the opportunities you are able to pursue.

Chapter 5: Make Income with Your Extra Space

Many people head into retirement in the same home, and they've lived in for several years. It is likely that if you have a family, you're going to have more than one room in your home. If your children are all grown up and moved into homes of their own, what do you do with all that extra space? Rent it out on vacation and holiday home rental platforms! It's the perfect solution for those looking to bring in a little extra cash during your retirement years! If you do not want to relocate from your family home this is just the ticket to bring in extra income from your space rather than downsize!

If you've got a beautiful, comfortable and cozy home which is conveniently located (public transport close by, city not too far away, easily commute to several locations without taking too much time), vacation home rental platforms like AirBnB, HomeAway and VRBO now present you with the option of putting that spare room(s) in your house to good use.

Getting Acquainted with AirBnB
AirBnB is today hands down one of the most popular online platforms that help connect individuals looking to rent out their spare rooms or spare homes even with people who are looking for more affordable accommodation as an alternative to expensive hotels. Since it was founded in 2008, the platform has now grown to cover more than 191 countries and 81,000 cities across the globe. In case you're

wondering how the name AirBnB came about, the hosts derived the name from "air mattress B&B (bed and breakfast).

The platform's popularity can be attributed to its win-win situation. For the hosts listing their properties for rent, it is a way to bring in a little extra from the spare rooms or homes they might not be using. For guests who are looking to rent, AirBnB provides a more inexpensive option. The slight risk that needs to be taken into account is that the AirBnB home might not be as nice or fantastic as the host made it out to be.

Before you jump at the chance to rent out that spare room or vacation home, here's what you need to consider before listing your property on the platform:

• **Rental Arbitrage Exists -** This is going to exist in every market for all short-term rental options. Arbitrage is the practice of earning a profit from the price difference between two or more markets by matching imbalanced deals. In simpler terms, you're essentially subletting to earn a profit. Here's a quick example to illustrate. Let's say you rent a house for $1000 a month and you list your home on Airbnb. You charge $100 a day. In 10 days you already got your rent. Rental arbitrage is exactly what makes AirBnB hosting so viable, but what you're going to need to bear in mind is that not all markets are the same. You're going to need to assess to what extent and viable your area or property is and if it makes sense for you to list as an AirBnB host profit wise. Also, it should be noted that if you're a renter, you'll need to check with your landlord about subletting rules.

- **What Type of Host Are You? -** Or what type of host do you intend to be for your guests? AirBnB hosts can be divided into three main categories. The first consists of homeowners who are just looking to make some extra cash with their spare rooms or second home. The second category is hosts who want to build a stable source of secondary income. The third group of hosts is those who are serious about turning their AirBnB business into a main source of income. If you're someone who can't stand the idea of having strangers in your home, or if you're a hoarder, anti-social or simply do not have the time commitment needed to host, then perhaps becoming an AirBnB host might not be the best approach for you. Many hosts alter their homes to have access from a private entrance into in-law suites or extra basement apartments. This provides privacy for the guests and the hosts. You can even use a self checkin system to allow access without personally checking each guest in.

- **You Need to Put in the Work -** It isn't going to be as simple as listing your home, uploading appealing pictures and then sitting back and waiting for the money to come in. You're going to need to invest the time to talk to potential guests, respond to all the questions asked and earn great reviews for your listing. If you rent a room inside your home, you may need to be there when the guests check in and out. Reading reviews of guests on airbnb and only booking to guests with great reviews from other hosts makes it safe process. Make sure that your property is clean and equipped with everything that you mentioned in your listing. Using Airbnb or other platforms in your your retirement years is great because you can communicate with guests online from your phone and be home or away in most cases. You can contract a cleaning service or ad a friend as a co host, to help with issues when you are away.

• **Know Your Size Before You Price** - If you wouldn't consider leaving your job before knowing what your new job is going to pay you, you shouldn't list your home before knowing exactly the price that it's worth. Mismatched prices are how you end up losing customers or making less than you should. For example, if you were making $2000 a month in AirBnB earnings but you were located in a high demand area, you could be making so much more than that and not even realizing it. **AirDNA** is a site every potential AirBnB host should check out before listing their property. It provides extensive and detailed data for almost all the major markets covered by AirBnB, and you'll get a more realistic gauge of what you could potentially make renting out your property in the market you're located in. Easily check the prices in your area by searching the site as a potential renter and you will see the properties in your area and what they are asking in rent, cleaning fees and other fees.

- **Get Your Insurance Sorted Out** - To be on the safe side, you should ensure that you've got your insurance coverage is adequate.It is unlikely that your current home insurance plan is going to cover damages caused by short term renting, so additional insurance might be required. A quick read through of AirBnB's liability insurance policy will let you know if the coverage is good to go or whether you might need more.

- **Remember Your Neighbors** - Noise complaints could kill your AirBnB business before you know it. Regardless of whether you're living in a community or a standalone home, you must be considerate of your neighbors and be clear about the rules regarding noise levels on your listing.

- **Prepare Your Amenities** - To provide the best experience for your guests , and make them so happy they'll be delighted to give you a rave review, your home needs to be equipped with the necessary amenities. Furniture is a serious consideration if you're thinking about making this a business. Your goal is to and mimic all the basic amenities which are provided by a hotel, and even what *you* might like to have if you were renting someone else's room for a short holiday. Adding a microwave and small refrigerator and desk to a room makes it much more appealing to a guest than just a private room.

Step-by-Step Guide to Listing on AirBnB

Platforms like AirBnB are popular not just because of what they offer, but also how easy to navigate and user-friendly their site can be. Once you're ready to list your property on AirBnB, your profile can easily be set up within a couple of minutes. Here's a quick overview!

• **Step 1: Creating An Account.** If you don't already have an account, create one by heading to the website. Select the "List Your Space" option located at the top right corner of the website's homepage and fill in the required criteria.

• **Step 2: Filling In the Details.** You'll be asked to provide details such as home type, city, and how many people your home accommodates. You'll want to be as specific with the details as possible.

• **Step 3: Choosing Your Availability.** You'll have three options to choose from. You could choose to list your property One Time (which is for a single or fixed time period), Sometimes (only on specific dates) or Always (listing indefinitely).

• **Step 4: Set Your Price.** AirBnb will provide you with suggestions of how much you should charge. This will be based on the information you keyed in about the details of your home. If you're doing this for the first time, AirBnB themselves recommend that you start pricing below the suggested rate as you work on building your profile and credentials. However, it is entirely up to you what price point you choose to go with. Some hosts factor in the cost of cleaning and utilities into their prices, although AirBnB does provide you with the option of adding a cleaning fee to your price.

• **Step 5: Make a Great Impression With Your Title.** This is what's going to capture your audience's attention, and with only 35 characters to work with, you should aim to make each word count. Consider using pleasant adjectives or descriptives, but avoid exaggerating.

• **Step 6: Create a Great Summary.** You've got 250 characters to work with here, and you should aim to write a fantastic summary that succinctly depicts your property and why guests should stay here. Aim for short, easy to read sentences, especially bullet points, because they're much easier to read.

• **Step 7: Upload Beautiful Pictures.** Aim for at least 10 pictures as the right balance between having too much and too little. The first 3 pictures on your profile are especially important because your pictures will be the deciding factor for your guests. High-quality images which stand out are the way to go.

- **Step 8: Listing Your Location.** The final step is listing your location. After filling out the details of your location, AirBnB will then proceed to prompt you a section to add directions to your property.

Once you're happy with the details of the listing, hit the publish button and you're all set with your AirBnB listing.

Listing Your Home on HomeAway

HomeAway and VRBO (Vacation Rental By Owner) cater to a more select type of property rentals, namely beach homes, condos, and cabins in the past. However, even some hotels now advertise their room locally on the platforms on VRBO and HomeAway. They currently cover over 2 million homes in 190 countries. This makes finding the perfect vacation home simple and easy! If you've already got that vacation home that's hardly being used, even after your retirement, why not list it on this platform and make a little extra income while you're at it?

HomeAway is part of the Expedia Group of family brands, and VRBO is just one of the many brands that fall under HomeAway family. Others include Homelidays, Abritel, FeWo, Bookabach, and Stayz.com.au. Founded in 2005 by Carl Shepherd and Brian Sharples, HomeAway and its brands aim to provide travelers with an affordable vacation home for rent which costs less than what it would for a hotel.

The motivating factor of the focus of HomeAway and VRBO specifically on vacation homes and properties is because they believe in cherishing those moments that bring a family together. They provide travelers with a place to escape from the hectic routine of those long work hours at the sacrifice of spending time with their families. Thus, HomeAway and VRBO strive to make planning and booking a family vacation as simple and hassle-free as possible.

With HomeAway and VRBO, homeowners have the tools insights and all the data that they need to provide the best experience for their guests. When you list your property, you set your own price points, the available dates, and the rules for the house. The platform provides a 23/7 support team which is on standby to help make sure everything goes smoothly for you should you need any help.

Step-By-Step Guide to Listing on HomeAway and VRBO

You know the basics of what it takes to rent what is considered the ideal property on AirBnB, and HomeAway and VRBO are no different. The idea is to make your property look as appealing as possible.

- **Step 1: Creating An Account.** If you don't already have an account, you'll need to create one by heading to the website. Again, the List Your Property button will be located at the top right hand corner of your screen.

- **Step 2: Filling In the Details.** Be as specific as possible with your listing details. Mention what's unique about the property.

- **Step 3: Pictures, Pictures, Pictures.** Aim for at least 10 pictures, just like with the AirBnB platform, so it's not too much, not too little, but just right.

- **Step 4: Connecting With Your Match.** HomeAway and VRBO will then connect you with travelers and help you find the perfect match for your property.

What's The Difference Between the Platforms?

All three platforms essentially work on the same concept, which is to rent out your extra space.

AirBnB - Why It's for You

This platform is a commerce site where hosts can personally upload and list their room or property for rent. Travelers then head over to the platform and book it directly themselves. AirBnB's unique offering lies in that you are able to choose from any type of property, where it's a room, a studio, a shared house, a home, and more. If you've got the space and there's someone willing to rent it, you're in business.

AirBnB is the perfect solution for travelers and hosts who love meeting people and are looking for a place to stay with people who are locals of the area. Especially travelers from abroad who wouldn't mind a friendly host showing them around the city. Some hosts even go the extra mile by helping to plan their itineraries, arrange for a local interpreter, driver, offer suggestions of where to even, and even go so far as to pick their guests up from the airport. It also offers privacy to guests by having whole homes and private spaces with separate entrances to guests who prefer not to interact.

VRBO - Why It's For You

If you're looking for a getaway that is extra special, the VRBO is the one for you. Even the word 'vacation' is in its name. What sets this one apart from AirBnB is that there are no listings for shared spaces, and if you're keen on exclusivity and privacy during your vacation with your family, this is the ideal solution since you'll have the entire home to yourself. Definitely cheaper than booking a hotel for the entire family at times, but you might miss out on certain amenities that come with hotel bookings, like a swimming pool or kids club for example. However many homes offer pool and other amenities! If you love large family get togethers, VRBO is where you should book your next vacation home.

HomeAway - Why It's For You

Since they're part of the same family, HomeAway works similarly to VRBO, with the option of choosing beach houses, condos, and cabins as your preferred home for your holiday. HomeAway has acquired over 20 companies since it was formed (VRBO included) to take the stress out of planning and searching for vacation rentals on multiple platforms by providing a one-stop solution for everything you need. Since only private homes are listed on this platform, you get to enjoy all the privacy you need without sharing a home with your host (that sometimes happens on AirBnB, especially if you're renting a room). Since HomeAway and VRBO are the same family, all the listings are shared across the platforms, saving you the hassle of cross-checking prices. At the time of this printing these two sites are merging to one for travelers (VRBO) and one for Owners (HomeAway).

All three of these platforms can be used simultaneously by an owner to take advantage of both markets.

BONUS TIP: Declutter Your Home for Cash While Starting Your AirBnb or VRBO business
Now that you're retired (or if you're about it), you've probably for some time to look around things you've accumulated over the years. If you're thinkingsome of the clutter has got to go, you'll be delighted to know that you could turn some of that clutter into cash! Take a look at these tips on selling your old items!

- **Kids Toys and Clothing -** Consignment stores are great for these, especially if you're selling them off in a bundle.

- **Gazelle and Envirofone** - These two sites will pay you cash for your old mobiles, laptops, and tablets. Gazelle buys almost anything from Apple, and you could make some good money depending on how new or old your tech is.

- **Decluttr.com -** Sell your old DVDs and CDs in exchange for some money, as long as they still work.

- **CraigsList, eBay and Amazon -** Perfect

for big-ticket items, like furniture for example. Newer items that you may have bought but never used could fetch a good price on these sites too, especially if you've never used them before.

•   **AbesBooks** - Instead of throwing those old books away, see if you could make some money of them by selling them to second-hand book sites like AbesBooks.

•   **Online Yard Sale on Facebook** - Join the Online Yard Sale Facebook group, it's like having a yard sale all the time, except you're doing it online.

Chapter 6: Introduction to Social Media Marketing

It cannot be denied that social media and its impacts have transcended almost every aspect of your life. From everyday happenings that we post about ourselves on our own platforms to updates about work, breaking news, even politics, most of our first-hand information these days seem to come from social media channels. So big has its impact and influence become that just about every big name brand and company out there is now relying on this new form of marketing to spread the word about their business. This new form of marketing is known as social media marketing.

Social media marketing is exactly what it sounds like. You market your products and services on *social media* websites instead of taking out an add in the local paper or other traditional advertising. If you're wondering how posts and status updates could qualify as 'marketing tactics,' it's because these updates include information, eye-catching images that are sure to get noticed, and updates about product information. Every piece of information has been carefully crafted and selected specifically to drive up engagement among the targeted audience. *That's* how online marketing works! Almost all social media platforms today will offer some form of paid advertising function, evidence that these platforms recognize their value to the marketing world.

Every business worth their salt knows how valuable social media marketing is for their business to exist and keep up with the demands of today's consumer. Brands now rely on social media platforms to announce new promotions, connect with audiences, and actively disseminate information which could boost their sales figures. Anyone who intends to own or run a business, online or otherwise, *needs* to start leveraging on social media marketing not just to raise brand awareness, but more importantly, to *connect* with your customers.

Consumers today are all about the connection. Nothing puts off a consumer more than a business who rarely responds to their queries or complaints. Customers are reaching out to business through DMs (direct messages) and social media more so than any other communication outlets. It's not an exaggeration to say that social media today is crucial for a business' survival, and here are the four primary reasons why:

- **Reason #1: Raise Brand Awareness** - With 3.2 billion people globally on social media as of 2018, a business simply cannot afford to miss out on this kind of exposure. This helps raise brand awareness because of the social engagement aspect that the platform provides. It enables direct two-way communication between both brand and customer through comments, likes, DMs and post shares. It may not seem like much, but these little connections make a big difference in fostering brand loyalty among your customers. They want brands who are responsive, brands whom they feel care about their needs and listen to their wants. Social media affords you the chance to show that *you are that brand* by communicating with them directly like you would if you were reaching out to a friend. Additionally, it also gives your brand a boost and directs traffic to your website through the links that you post on your content.

- **Reason #2: Building Relationships -** Closely linked with Reason #1 is building relationships. Businesses today have a unique opportunity. They are able to bridge the gap between brand and consumer by connecting with their customers in a way they never could before. Traditional marketing was merely an ad you saw on your television, listen to on the radio or read about in the local newspaper. That was it. The company was still a distant, cold being that you knew very little about. Not today, though. Today customers can interact with their favorite brands almost as if those businesses were their next door neighbor. More like the days when we had local stores who offered personalized service because everyone in the community knew each other! With behind the scenes footage, live video broadcastings as it's happening and responses received within mere minutes of posting them on social media, businesses now have the opportunity to take their relationship with their customers to the next level. By communicating with them on a level that they understand, reaching out to them and managing

70

their expectations, you effectively foster brand loyalty by getting the customers to feel a connection to you.

• **Reason #3: Lead Generation -** Social media has given you the simplest tool available to help you improve your lead generation, increase sales and boost conversions. A 'lead' is a potential customer who has given an indication that they *may* be interested in what your business is offering. This lead is a potential sale in the making, and if you actively engage with them on social media, subtly convincing them why your products or services are right for them, you'll be able to turn that lead into a converted customer. Whenever you create a contest on your social media profile, you're encouraging lead generation. When you include links on your profile which lead back to your website, you're encouraging lead generation. You can learn more about all these aspects by researching the topic online!

• **Reason #4: Your Competitors -** You always need to know what your competition is up to. What campaigns are they running? How do they post their content on social media? What tactics and strategies are they employing? How are they interacting with their customers? Stay one step ahead of the competition by taking notice of what they do and try improve upon that! Since social media is out there for all the world to see, you'll easily be able monster your competition!

You could even learn a thing or two about how to improve your own marketing tactics by observing what works well for your competitors.

All this new information can be overwhelming if you are not acquainted with social media! So let's talk a little about where to start!

I've Never Made A Facebook or Instagram Post In My Life! Where Do I Begin?

Anything that's new can seem challenging at first. Perhaps even a little daunting. With no clue where to begin or how to get started, it is easy to feel overwhelmed and stressed out pretty quickly. Social media marketing seems to may have been dominated by the young, but that doesn't mean you can't quickly catch up too if you're a retiree. In fact, learning how to get the hang of social media platforms is easier than you think, especially when they're so intuitive and interactive. Platforms like Facebook and Instagram have made it so easy for you to get anything done with their step-by-step prompts which tell you what action needs to be taken next, so there's no reason to worry at all. Not in the least.

If you're new to this whole social media marketing concept, it won't be long before you learn to navigate your way around. It helps alot to create personal account on the social media you want to use. Then explore it as a potential customer. Before long you are keeping up with friends as well as seeing ads pop up to advertise to YOU based on your interests. Soon you will learn by doing and then you can start to market your business on social media platforms. To make the process a little easier, it is recommended that you complete the following steps:

• **Step 1: Choosing Your Goals to Optimize -** You're likely to have several goals laid out for your business, and you want to accomplish every one of them immediately. However, trying to manage too many things at once can often backfire. Instead of perfecting two or three goals by giving them your 100% attention, you're left with five goals with the mediocre outcome because you weren't able to give each goal as much attention as it needed. You need to pick at least one or two goals that you want to optimize and working on those first before moving onto anything else. Basing your goals on the SMART approach is the best way to begin since this framework helps you define exactly what you should be working on. **S**pecific goals which are **M**easurable and **A**chievable, **R**esults-oriented and **T**ime-sensitive, are far more definitive that vague goals that simply say *I want to increase my social media following.* Using the SMART approach, that sentence would read, *I want to increase my Facebook following to 500 followers within four months through social media contests and promotions.* Notice the difference?

• **Step 2: Defining Your Objectives** - Go back to the points discussed earlier how social media could help raise brand awareness, forge relationships, encourage lead generation and help you keep abreast of what your competitors are doing. Those are your *objectives* and what you should be basing your social media strategy on. Just like the goals, you want to work on picking one or two at a time, so you don't run the risk of spreading yourself far too thin. If you're a new business, one of the first objectives you should be focusing on would be building awareness, and once you've determined that, you can then go about mapping out the steps towards getting that done.

• **Step 3: Find Out Who Your Audience Is -** You can't run a business or a marketing campaign for that matter, without knowing *who* your target audience is. You wouldn't drive a car without knowing where you're going, and your social media marketing strategy is based along with the same principle. Know who your audience is and know who you're talking to. Are they young millennials in their 20s and 30s? The older generation? Those about to retire or already retired like yourself? Knowing whose attention you're trying to grab will make it much easier for you to determine the kind of content you should craft. Explore Facebook and Instagram and do a little digging about the demographics that you have in mind. How often are they online? How much time do they spend on social media? What sort of products or services are they looking for? How do they engage with similar content like the ones you intend to post?

- **Step 4: Engaging Content -** Your content needs to be unique, engaging, and interesting to your target audience. Your customers are very likely not just going to be following you; they're going to be following your competitors too. They'll be comparing your content against that of your competition, and if your content isn't as unique and engaging, you're going to find yourself losing followers fast. Avoid the temptation to post just for the sake of having something to post on your profile. Invest the time needed to curate the necessary content, look at what your competitors are doing for some inspiration, and think about what you could do better.

- **Step 5: Scheduling Your Content -** Putting all that time and effort into creating great content, naturally, you'd want it to be seen by as many people as possible. More importantly, you don't want to skip out on missing a post because you were occupied with other tasks and before you know it, the entire day has gone by and you've just realized oh no! You forgot to put the content you were supposed to. Social media management tools that help you schedule and prepare your content ahead of time and post according to the plan are a lifesaver. Not only do these tools help you post your content on time, they enable you to monitor the interactions and engagement you get per post. This saves you lots of time in the process, time which could be spent either focusing on your business or creating the next piece of exciting content. Hootsuite, HubSpot, SproutSocial are three great examples of social media management tools that are effective, and you should definitely consider these as an option if you want to get serious about your social media marketing tactics.

How Often Should I Be Posting on Social Media?
The general rule of them is posting only when you have content of quality to share, but you don't want to leave such a long gap between posts either. Posting once a day is good enough as long as the content has the quality to it. Posting far too infrequently leaves you at risk of being forgotten by your followers, maybe even losing followers in the process. However, posting far too often also puts you at risk of annoying your followers since they see this as "spamming" their newsfeed.

HubSpot has an excellent resource showing you just how often you should post based on the industry that you're in. Since not all businesses are created equal, it's a good idea to research your industry standards benchmark to give you some idea about how to get started. Later you could begin experimenting with posts of your own and gauge the levels of engagement that you are receiving per content.

Analyzing Your Social Media Impact
When you organize any sort of campaign, you want to see the outcome and how effective that campaign was at delivering the results you wanted. Social media marketing works in the same way. To assess the results and the impact of each campaign that you organize, you will need to keep a close watch on all your posts on every single platform

you operate. If you're running on Facebook and Instagram, keep tabs on each piece of content across both those platforms. This is easily done by managing and reviewing what is known as your social media metrics.

These metrics are the data which is related to the success of your content and provides you detailed information about how impactful your content was with your audience. The metrics could include various forms of data like engagement levels, number of likes and shares, how many people are following your profile and your content, among other things. As a beginner, all this information may seem overwhelming but don't worry, all you need to do to get started is to keep tabs on the following 10 metrics, because they are the most important:

- Engagement levels
- Reach
- Followers
- Impressions
- Number of visits to your profile
- Number of mentions
- How many times your content gets reposted
- How many times your content gets shared
- Number of video views you're garnering

Measuring these analytics is not as complicated as you might think, because once again, social media platforms themselves have made things easy by providing you with the analytics tools that you need inbuilt into the platform. On Facebook, it's referred to as Facebook Analytics and on Instagram, what you're looking for is Instagram Insights.

How Do I Use These Social Media Platforms to Place My Ads? Here is an Overview!

When you have your social media platform up and running, it's time to put it to good use by marketing your business and services. Let's say you've decided becoming an AirBnB host. Getting your listing noticed by as many people as possible means that it has to be posted on social media.

AirBnB has made it easy for you to list your property on various other social media platforms. In four simple steps, your listing could be up and running on Facebook and Instagram, reading to be seen by thousands who may be looking for a home just like yours. To list your AirBnB on Facebook and Instagram, here's what you would need to do:

- Step 1: Go to the AirBnB website and select 'Manage Listings'
- Step 2: Select the listing that you would like to share (if you have more than one listing)
- Step 3: Under your listing page, there will be a '**Save to Wishlist**' option and three dots (...) which are accompanied by a '**More**' option. Click on it.
- Step 4: Simply select the social media platform (Facebook or Instagram) that you would like to share this listing on and follow the next few prompts to complete the process.

Voila! Listing is done.

Now, let's say that you wanted to create a Facebook ad to market your business, products or services and broaden your reach to get your clients. Business LOVE Facebook ads because of how affordable and inexpensive they are compared to the traditional types of advertising mediums they had to rely on before. Here's a step-by-step of how to set up your very first Facebook Ad:

- Step 1: Head to your Facebook Ads Manager (you will need to have a Facebook page for this, not a personal profile).
- Step 2: Choose the objective of your ad campaign. Remember the objectives which were defined earlier? Page likes, video views, higher engagement levels and more? If your objective for your ad was to promote your page, you would select the 'Promote your Page' option.

(Image via HubSpot)

- Step 3: Narrow down who your target audience is so your ad reaches the exact group of people that you want. This is where knowing who your target audience is, their behavior patterns, demographics and interests will help you out.

(Image via HubSpot)

- Step 4: Choose your budget from the two options Facebook provides, which would be the Daily Budget (minimum daily amount starts at $1.00), or the Lifetime Budget.
- Step 5: Determine your ad schedule by selecting whether you want your

campaign to begin running immediately, of if you would prefer more customized start and end dates.

•   Step 6: It's time to pick the right format for your ad. The options you have to work with include photo, video, carousel, slideshow, collection, canvas, lead ads, dynamic ads and link ads. Have a quick read through about what each option does and determine which would be best suited to help you achieve the objectives that you want.

Once you're satisfied with your ad, hit the publish button and you're done.

Instagram Ads are just as easy to set up and you could be marketing your business and services in mere minutes. Just like Facebook, Instagram ads come in several options to choose from, including photo ads, video ads, carousel ads, Stories ads and canvas stories ads. You'll need to familiarize yourself with the different ad options and once again, revisit your objects to determine which ad type is going to be best to achieve the outcome you want. Once done, here are the next steps to quickly set up your very first Instagram ad:

•   Step 1: You will need to connect your Instagram account to a Facebook Business Page (it is recommended that you set up your Facebook business page first before getting started on Instagram).

•   Step 2: If you've already got your Facebook business profile set up, go to the Business Manager section on Facebook.

•   Step 3: On the left of the page, choose the 'Business Settings' option. The choose 'Instagram Accounts'.

•   Step 4: Click on 'Claim New Instagram Account' and add your username and password. Click 'Next' when you're done.

•   Step 5: Approve the authorizations and save the changes made.

•   Step 6: Choose your ad objective, just like what you did with Facebook. Do you want to increase brand awareness? Boost your reach? Encourage more engagement?

•   Step 7: Target your audience based on their demographics (just like on Facebook).

•   Step 8: Decide where your ads are going to appear by making the appropriate selections in the 'Placement' section. Ads will show up on the platforms which they are most likely to perform well if you choose 'Automatic Placements.'

•   Step 9: Determine your budget and how much you're willing to spend. This will be based on how long you intend to run the ad for. You have the same two options to choose from, which are the Daily Budget or Lifetime Budget.

- Step 10: Time to create your ad with an interesting, catchy headline followed by an equally interesting description. Don't forget about using high-quality images.

- Step 11: Add a call to action button to drive your audience to take action. You would have seen these buttons on just about every ad on your own social media feeds. Shop Now, Call Now, Like Now are some examples of the call to action buttons you could use, depending on your ad content.

When you're satisfied with how everything looks, click on the 'Confirm' button, and you're done. Congratulations! You have now learned how to successful list ads promoting your business and services on social media. Don't worry. It gets easier and quicker to list your content once you get used to it. You'll be breezing through the steps before you know it. You can refer to these steps when you are actually ready to go through the process.

Chapter 7: Dotting the I's and Crossing the T's

The truth is, all of us are going to die one day. As hard as that may be to hear, it's still doesn't make it less of a fact. Nobody likes to think about their death, but now that you're retired (or about to retire), it's something you're going to have to start putting some serious thought into for the sake of your family. Not only does it make things much easier for you to have your affairs in order, but you also make it much easier for the family, especially when you don't leave them with a lot of debt to clear once everything's said and done. Its a great legacy and blessing to leave your family with little to do to settle your estate when your time on earth is over.

Why Do We Need to Think About Such a Gloomy Affair?
We all love our families and love motivates us to plan ahead so that they are not stressed at a time of grieving in their lives.You would have likely accumulated several possessions and assets throughout the course of your life, and you need to think about what's going to happen to it all when you're no longer around. There's a lot more work that goes into taking care of your affairs than you may realize, and the sooner you get started, the less stress and rush involved. The more assets or possessions you own, the longer it may take (depending on how quickly you can work through everything). It is best to enlist the help of a lawyer when it comes to the preparation and managing of your will, distribution of big assets and the general

planning of your estate. Some legal services like LegalShield will prepare your wills and offer certain legal services for a small monthly membership.

When planning for what's going to happen after your death, you need to focus on two specific areas. The first is what happens after death (obviously), and the second is what happens *if you fall ill and you're unable to handle* or make any important decisions on your own. Let's look into the first part first, and it begins with your last will and testament.

What Is A Last Will and Testament and How Do I Prepare One?

There will be *two* types of wills which you will need to prepare. One is called a *living will*, and the other is, of course, your last will and testament. We'll discuss the living will shortly after this.

This is a document which is going to decide what's going to happen to all your worldly possessions after your death. This includes property that you own, any financial balances which may be left over, and even the guardianship of any young children under your care. The document should also name who will be the executor of your will, which is the person who will bear the responsibility of carrying out your final wishes after your death. Depending on how much property or possessions you own, your will could either be simple or more detailed. Naturally, the less you own, the simpler the document will be.

If you're wondering whether it would be possible for you to draft up a simple copy of your own will, the answer is yes, but there are both pros and cons that come with it. The cons include the possibility of outdated information, details about how specific trust issues should be handled or even issues with missing details regarding your taxes, given that you would have had little to no prior experience about how a will should be prepared. While the option to prepare your wills online does exist, it's not a very effective approach because the documents available online are more of a one-size-fits-all approach. These documents are prepared for general mass use, and they're unlikely to account for how complicated real-life situations can become. Again, of course, it depends entirely on the kind of document that you need. If you don't own a lot, and you're unmarried with no next of kin to leave your belongings too, then a simple will is probably going to suffice.

It is very important not to leave out the details of who should be the executor of your will. This person will have a very big responsibility on their hands, and you'll want to pick someone that you can trust wholeheartedly to ensure that your final wishes are carried out exactly as you want them to be. The most common and obvious choice would be your immediate next of kin, which would be either children or other family members. The executor of your last will and testament will be responsible for handling your estate (all the property that you're leaving behind, if any), as well as the handling of your remaining finances, any debts which may have been leftover and all other matters that need to be taken care of now that you're no longer around. The executor will only have power and control over your estate *after* your death and not before since the document is not effective until after your death.

Deciding What to Do If You Become Incapacitated

In the event you become ill or incapacitated, which renders you unable to perform any important decisions, you need to determine what's going to happen should such a scenario play out. This is the reason why you're going to need to prepare two different types of will, and this *living will* is the document where you will appoint a power of attorney, both regular and medical. The prospect of preparing one in the event you might become too sick to carry out your own affairs sounds frightening, but it is better to be prepared than not to be.

The first thing you need to do is designate a power of attorney for your living will. This person will be responsible for overseeing your legal and financial matters in the event that you can't do them yourself. It is better to have this person already appointed beforehand so that should you fall ill, they will be prepared to immediately take over and attend to any financial and legal matters which need to be sorted out. This person will only have the power of attorney as long as you're alive, and their role will cease immediately upon your death. The power then shifts to the executor that you appointed in your will. Depending on your preference, the person who is acting as your power of attorney can also be the executor of your will if that is your choice.

There are several options of what you could go with when it comes to power of attorney (medical, general, limited, durable). You could look into the available options to familiarize yourself with the roles and responsibilities that come with the position, but an enduring power of attorney might be one of the top choices for you to consider. Enduring power of attorney falls under the Durable Power of Attorney option, and it sometimes referred to as *power of attorney with durable provisions*. This option might be the best approach to consider because the power of attorney goes into effect as soon as you sign your legal documents and will continue to remain effective until your death. This means that when you sign your document, this person is going to be able to immediately access all your legal and financial matters as soon as you have been declared either incapacitated or incompetent.

This living will of yours will essentially be your healthcare directive which you are preparing in advance. This document will contain in detail what your wishes are for medical care, just in case you have fallen so ill that you are no longer able to speak for yourself. It might be helpful to get a lawyer at this stage to walk you through the process and explain in detail anything you may not be sure of. It is very important that you be clear about every single aspect covered in preparing your living will.

Ordinary Power of Attorney vs Lasting Power of Attorney

It was mentioned that there are several options to choose from when it comes to deciding on your power of attorney. Besides the Durable Power of Attorney, there are two others which you should make a note of, which is the Ordinary Power of Attorney and Lasting Power of Attorney.

An Ordinary Power of Attorney is a designated person who

will be responsible for handling your financial affairs. They come into power in the event you experience any sort of mental incapacitation which renders you unable to make any important financial decisions on your own. This form of power of attorney is useful in temporary situations, such as when you may be hospitalized for a period, when you're ill and find it hard to leave your home to go to the bank and you want someone to help you access your account, or if you want someone to act on your behalf while you observe their actions.

With an Ordinary Power of Attorney, more than one person could be appointed to make these financial decisions on behalf of you. You are able to limit your attorney's power if you wish so that they only deal with some of your assets instead of all of it. This power of attorney is only valid *as long as you have the mental capacity to still make decisions on your own*. Should you want someone to act on your behalf when you can no longer make these decisions, that's where the Lasting Power of Attorney comes in.

A Lasting Power of Attorney (LPA) is a designated person who will handle decisions regarding your financial affairs or matters related to your health care. This power of attorney also comes into effect in the event you become mentally incapacitated. Your LPA needs to be someone that you can trust, especially since you're giving them all the legal authority that they need to make decisions on your behalf in the future.

An LPA who is overseeing your financial decisions can still be of use to you while you have your mental capacity unless you state that you only want them to come into effect when you lose this mental capacity. They will be responsible for decisions which include financial investments, mortgage payments, bill payments, and any sale or purchase of the property. You can choose to let them make all of these decisions for you on your behalf, or you could choose to limit the authority that they have to certain decisions only. Your LPA must keep tabs on all your accounts and their money kept separate from yours. You have the right to ask for regular details regarding how much of your money is left and what has been spent. In the event you lose your mental capacity, these details can be revealed to a family member or your designated solicitor.

When appointing an LPA for health and related medical decisions, the LPA can only come into effect *after* you have lost mental capacity. This person will be responsible for handling decisions which include your medical care, your living situation, the nutrition that you should receive, which you will be contacting and even the types of social activities that you should or should not participate in. An LPA may also be given special permission to make decisions which involve life-saving treatments for you.

Making the Funeral Arrangements
While this step is optional if you want to make things easier for your family members who will already be grieving your loss, take the added burden off their shoulders by planning and preparing for your own funeral service, including the memorial arrangements. If you do decide to go with this route, remember to put it in writing and let your family know explicitly that this is what you

want them to do and these are your wishes.

Should you want to outline your own preparations for this process, here are the areas that you could cover:

- If you would like a burial, then you will need to find a designated grave plot, which can easily be done by contacting your preferred local cemetery and purchase an available plot.

- If you would like a cremation instead, you could get in touch with a local funeral home and sort out the arrangement details with them.
- Plan the details of what and how you would like your wake to be handled if you've got something specific in mind. Get it in writing and let your family members know to about these too.

To alleviate your family's financial burden, a good option to consider would be to pre-pay for the arrangements that you make ahead of time. That way, your family will not have to worry about paying for anything once the funeral is over.

Funeral costs, however, don't come cheap. In fact, as of 2017, the National Funeral Director's Association has outlined the median of what a funeral would cost, and the numbers are as follows:
- Basic funeral home service fee: $2,100
- Embalming & preparation fee: $975
- Funeral ceremony: $500
- Metal casket: $2,400

- Vault: $1,395
- Cremation: $350
- Cremation casket: $1,000
- Urn: $275

The costs will vary, of course, depending on the arrangements that you choose to go with. Those costs don't yet include the cost to secure and prepare the plot for your burial, which could easily cost you anywhere between $1,000 to $2,000, not to mention the gravestone which will again put you out of another $1,500 to $2,000 on average.

To prepay as much as possible for your own funeral arrangements, you will need to create a plan. A plan which includes:

- **Getting Life Insurance** - This type of insurance policy could provide your family with some financial security if you earmark it specifically to cover the cost of your funeral. Nothing is harder than leaving family with your expense and cause them to struggle to pay for your final expenses!

- **Setting Up a Savings Account for Funeral Planning -** If you haven't retired yet, there's still time for you to set up a designated savings account specifically for your funeral costs. Aim to go with bank accounts which are going to provide you with the highest interest rates so your money is compounded by the time it's time to withdraw it.

Putting Things in Order: Organizing the Rest of Your Financial Affairs

The will that you prepare is mainly going to cover the bulk of the assets you own. There will still be other financial matters which you need to attend to, such as any outstanding bills, debts, insurance policies and even existing bank accounts, little details that still need to be organized and taken care of. Life insurance policies, retirement pensions and annuities especially, are the ones that most often get overlooked.

To get started organizing all your finances together, start by:

- **Consolidating Your Outstanding Debt**. This includes everything from mortgages to small bills like car loans or credit card bills, for example. If you owe money somewhere, even if it is so a person and not a bank, write it all down and have all of this laid out in a clear, precise order.

- **Organize This Debt In a Notebook** - Start keeping track of all your debt payments from this point on. The best way to do this is by keeping tabs of every single payment in a neat, systematic manner. If you love working with excel spreadsheets, prepare a spreadsheet which documents all your debt and every payment which has been made up to the very latest one. Should you prefer the more traditional approach, write it all down in a notebook (not pieces of paper which might get misplaced). No matter which approach you choose to go with, remember that it needs to easily be accessible to your remaining family members when the time comes so that they know exactly what debts are left, how much has been paid, who it gets paid to and what the outstanding balance is.

• **Don't Forget About The Digital Stuff -** We often forget that so much of our life is online these days that it needs to be organized and ready to be handed over to the next of kin too. This means any and all existing, active online accounts that you have must be consolidated and listed out systematically too. Names of websites or accounts, along with the passwords must be kept in a systematic fashion so that it is easy for the next person to know exactly what to do and how to log into your accounts should they need to.

• **Preparing a Master File -** Once you've got all your documents in order, including your will, it is now time to prepare what's known as a master file. This master file is going to be for your family, and it should contain *everything* about your life. That's not an exaggeration. This includes not just your will, but everything else from birth certificates, marriage certificates, citizenship documents, letter of instructions, divorce or separation documents, drivers licenses, names or healthcare professionals, military records if any, medications and their dosages, the name of the pharmacy and documents that you regularly use, addresses and phone numbers of your doctors and hospitals, source of income, all your accounts and passwords, ATM cards and pin numbers, financial assets, other assets, retirement accounts and every other important piece of information or document that has a big influence on your life. These records should be kept in a safe place like a security deposit box or safe of course, but at least one trusted family member should be notified of these documents and how to access them.

Leaving a list of your passwords and login details, along with bank account numbers and other sensitive information is a process which gets overlooked by many because we never think to share this sensitive information with anyone, not even our own family. But now is the time that it needs to get done, not just so that your family can have access to your accounts (both physical and digital), it also makes it easier for them to discontinue or shut down the services that are no longer needed after your death.

Do you have more than one source of income even after retirement? Consider setting an appointment with a financial advisor to help you figure out how best you can organize this. The advisor will be able to help you figure out how you can designate your beneficiaries, how to make your financial accounts accessible and even help you create a spending plan if you would like for your remaining family members if you're leaving them with a substantial amount of money.

Keeping Your Will Up to Date

Aim to update your will as often as you can, perhaps once every six months or once a year. You should always keep copies of your will as you update them to make it easier for you to review the changes which may or may not have been made. A will must be kept up to date to ensure that all your bases are covered. Things change, situations change, the property may have been bought or sold since your last will was prepared, or you may have had a change of heart even as time goes on, and updating your will to reflect this changes means that you are always prepared. Once you have updated your will to the most recent copy, you can then destroy old copies of the will to avoid any confusion from arising. There should always be only *one* legitimate and active copy of your will at all times.

How to Minimize Estate Taxes

Any property which is left by the deceased to their beneficiaries is subject to what is known as inheritance tax. Speaking to an attorney about this matter is a good investment!

With careful planning, you could minimize the impact of these taxes through the following measures:

- **Figure Out What's Taxable -** Securities, insurance, trust, real estate, annuities, cash and business interests are all considered taxable assets. You will need to refer to the Internal Revenue Services (IRS) Estate Tax Return form, Form 706, for detailed instructions to understand what is deemed taxable.

- **Figure Out What's Excluded -** Items which have been owned solely by others or spouses, life estates which have been given to you and the title passed along once you're deceased are generally not considered taxable.

- **Figuring Out The Estate You Own Is Taxable -** Back in 2016, the applicable federal exclusion came into effect to the tune of $5.45 million, which means that you would not be considered taxable if you do not exceed this amount. If you don't exceed the amount, you will not have to file an Estate Tax Return.

- **Setting Up an Estate Plan -** Not only does this help to minimize your taxes, but you also avoid family disagreements and having your remaining relatives fight over your property after your death.

Thinking About Your Options for Long-Term Care

There may come a time when you are no longer able to care for yourself, and you'll need to rely on long-term care options unless you're planning to live with a family member during the rest of your golden years. Some may cringe at the idea of a nursing home, but this could be a very real possibility which needs to be considered. You may need this at some point in your life, and the smart thing would be to start thinking about it as soon as possible.

Again, what a wonderful thing it is that we live in a world full of options and possibilities. A nursing home doesn't have to be your only option for long-term care anymore. You can now choose between assisted living, adult day care, home health care and even skilled nursing, depending on your needs. You've also got several options to consider in terms of how to pay for this long-term care, especially when you're running on limited funds:

- Check if your current insurance policy has you covered for long-term care. If it doesn't, consider insuring yourself for one.
- If you've got a high-deductible health plan, you could have access to a Health Savings Account (HSA). Check your current health care plan to determine if this is an option for you.
- If you're not already retired, the obvious answer is to start preparing from now and to start saving for it.
- You may be eligible for Medicaid, depending on the current state of your finances.
- Consider a combined life insurance policy that comes with long-term care benefits.
- Consider combining your annuity with long term care benefits

Chapter 8: Untold Saving Hacks For Retirees

How much time have you spent thinking about where you would want to live once you retire? Whether you've thought about it a lot or hardly ever (until now that it), where you choose to live has a big impact on your finances. It determines the quality of life you'll be able to afford, what sort of leisure activities you can indulge in, the kind of home you can afford, how much you'd need to cover your monthly expenses, even the kind of access to healthcare that you'll have. Where you retire is the biggest untold savings hack, and it is *the number one money-saving move* you could make. If the city that you're living in now is far too expensive and your retirement finances don't match up, why not think about moving to a cheaper city? Or a cheaper country even?

Many retirees today are open to the idea of moving abroad and retiring in a different country. It is not uncommon today to find Mr. and Mrs. Jones from New York now happily retired in Maldives or Thailand, living out their retirement dreams the way they've always wanted and more. Simply because they moved to a much more affordable, much cheaper place to live. Anyone who is looking for an affordable retirement needs to put this as an option. It makes sense to move to a location that is better suited to your needs and budget rather than have to stress about how long your retirement money is going to last you, or how you're going to afford a lot of things if you're retiring with less than what you should have. You might not like the idea of having to uproot or leave behind the home and lifestyle you've gotten so used to already, but if you were to find an option that is better suited to your interests and your budget, why not? After all, if you've dreamed about retiring in a beautiful vacation home somewhere, it's almost the same concept, except this time you're choosing somewhere more affordable to do it.

Okay, I'm Sold! What Should I Consider Before Moving?

The factors to look out for when deciding which country or city might be best suited to your retirement plans would be to look at it in terms of housing affordability, the quality of the healthcare available in that location, what the local job market is like, how desirable this country is when compared to others, whether there are any taxes imposed on retirees and of course, whether you're going to be happy living here or not. At least, that was the criteria that the **U.S. News** when it came to how they ranked the best places in the United States to retire and live in.

Let's take a look at the 10 best cities in the US to retire in as of 2019 based on the U.S News findings.

10 Best Cities to Retire in If You're Living in the U.S.

Whether you're already retired or about to retire, it's not too late to still live out all the retirement dreams that you've held inside you for so long, especially when these cities are going to make your everyday cost of living a lot more affordable:

#1 - Lancaster, Pennsylvania

The housing affordability is a major plus point, along with the many health care services which are available at the local Lancaster General Hospital. Retirees are looking at a median home price of about $198,500 based on data from the Census Bureau.

#2 - Daytona Beach, Florida

Living on a modest retirement income? Welcome to Daytona Beach, Florida, your new retirement abode where the median home price among those over 60 years old is $185,300 (Census Bureau). Health care is readily available at both the Florida Hospital Memorial Medical Center and the Halifax Health Medical Center. If you're worried about state income taxes, Florida doesn't have them, which makes a low cost of living for retirees even more affordable. Better yet if you intend to continue working part-time. For those who dream about retirement by the beach, this is the place to be.

#3 - Grand Rapids, Michigan

Art-loving retirees will love to call this place home since Grand Rapids is known for its reputation as an artist haven. Every fall the entire city transforms into an art gallery, and if you're keen on it, retirees could even think about taking up a volunteer position at the Grand Rapids Art Museum. The city provides several available health care options, and the median home price that you're looking at for those aged 60 and above is $171,100.

#4 - Melbourne, Florida

Another Florida favorite for those who have their heart set

on retiring by the beach would be Melbourne. Median home prices are in the $191,200 (Census Bureau) range for those 60 and above, and its affordable housing is one of the major reasons this city has become a quick favorite among retirees who are looking to spend their golden years in a much cheaper location. An interesting fact to note is that the city is also referred to as the Space Coast because of its close proximity to the Kennedy Space Center, and the Cape Canaveral Air Force Station.

#5 - *Jacksonville, Florida*
White-sandy beaches with Atlantic Ocean waves gently lapping on its shores and pleasantly mild winters are what's in store for you should you relocate to Jacksonville, Florida. It is known as a golfer's retirement haven, and some of its golf courses are renown for overlooking the ocean. The city is home to several hospitals which have been ranked as high-performing facilities, and the median home price you're looking at for those above 60 would be in the $200,800 range. Don't forget that Florida has no income tax, which is good news for those who still intend to work even after retirement.

#6 - *Fort Myers, Florida*
Probably a big reason why Florida keeps popping up as a desirable place to live would be the absence of taxes, which - when you're retired - is a major plus point to consider. Especially when you may have some taxable sources of income even after your retirement. For the retirees whose perfect retirement scenario includes boating, fishing, or simply just relaxing by the beach, Fort Myers is your new home. Despite its hot summers, the city has surprisingly

cool winters, and with a median home price of $233,100, the city is certainly an affordable place to consider spending the rest of your retirement days.

#7 - *Austin, Texas*
A city most famed for its quirky culture and live music, Austin is home to some of the world's major tech hubs, including the likes of Apple, Samsung, Dell, and IBM. Seton Medical Center and St. David's Medical Center is the city's biggest healthcare providers. For those who are interested in going back to school or taking up some college classes to brush up on your skills after retirement, you'll be happy to note that Austin is college town which welcomes retirees. Even those over the age of 65 and more could take up to six credit hours of courses at the local University of Texas-Austin, and the best part is that its tuition-free! The median home prices can be a little on the high side, hovering in the $283,500 range, but if you were to compare it to other similar coastal cities in the US, it is a considerably more affordable place to live.

#8 - *Portland, Maine*
Its rocky coastline is home to the most mesmerizing and breath-taking view of the Atlantic Ocean, an absolute dream for those who love the beach and want to spend the rest of their days overlooking such a beautiful sight. In terms of happiness, this city had the highest score based on the Gallup-Healthways survey outcome. Retirees are looking at a median home price of $265,000 to call this place their retirement home.

#9 - Raleigh & Durham, North Carolina

Another favorite for retirees who are looking to return to school once more is this city in North Carolina. For retirees aged 65 and older, the North Carolina State University provides you with the option of auditing courses for free at the university, as long as the course that you're doing is not a degree. In fact, one of its other universities, Duke University, has an existing retirement community located not too far from campus. It's highly educated community is the place to be to find like-minded individuals for those seeking to do something more after retiring. The median home price you're looking at is $249,294.

#10 - San Diego, California

It's convenient location next to the Pacific Ocean, the range of available health and medical options and the all year round pleasant and delightful weather is one of the many reasons San Diego is a favorite among retirees. In fact, the U.S. News survey found that the city was actually voted one of the most desirable places to live in the US, despite the biggest drawback of the city, which is the significantly higher housing costs. Especially when compared to all the other cities above. Retirees over 60 are looking at a whopping $560,200 as the median home price, although if you're willing to rent, you're looking at forking out the median rental costs, which is about $1,296 per month.

If you're looking for more options of locations to consider settling down in after retirement, **U.S News** is a great resource to go through, with key details that every retiree should be looking out for when surveying their next home to live in.

10 Best Places to Retire Abroad

Everyone would have a different picture of what their retirement would look like. Some could have their sights set on retiring abroad in a foreign land, seeing retirement as a new adventure. Or perhaps even to fulfill a dream they have had of living in a foreign land. When surveying countries that would make the best retirement destinations, several factors should be considered, including the cost of living, what the local climate was like, healthcare, visa and residency criteria, overall quality of life and how easy it would be to settle down once you've relocated.

These countries have been ranked by as among the best to retire abroad in, but of course, if there's a place that you've always wanted to go, you could do your own research into the reality of making that country your second home after retirement.

#1 - Spain
Millions of tourists' love flocking to this sunny city for its beautiful sandy beaches and its relaxed, laid back way of life. The country has a large English-speaking expat community, great healthcare system, and low cost of living compared to several other European countries.

#2 - Peru
Low cost of living, combined with its diverse and beautiful landscape comprising of jungles, beaches and mountains, Peru is famed for its many cultural activities and attractions, attracting more retirees over the years.

#3 - Thailand
Venturing a little further east is Thailand, where you'll find many retirees from all walks of life and all sorts of countries. Its year-long warm weather, beaches and bustling cities has always made it a top holiday destination for years. Now, it has become an equally popular retirement destination too.

#4 - Portugal
English is widely spoken in this friendly country, and living here is a lot more affordable compared to several other European nations. The Global Peace Index 2018 even ranked the country in fourth place, so be prepared to live a life that is relatively stress free.

#5 - Columbia
Besides is tropical climate, Columbia is growing in popularity among retirees because of its simple, hassle-free visa requirements. The country's healthcare system has been ranked 22nd in the world by the World Health Organization, and the affordable quality of life is drawing more expats to settle down in the country after retirement.

#6 - Malaysia
Renown for its good food, friendly people and year-round climate that is hot and humid, Malaysia has now become a popular retirement destination. English is widely spoken here, which makes it easy for retirees to settle into their new way of life quickly. Malaysia has the added benefit of both private healthcare, which is relatively low-cost and public healthcare, which is even more affordable.

#7- *Ecuador*

If you want quality, affordable healthcare and the benefit of being exempted from certain taxed, this tropical climate country is the place to be.

#8 - *Mexico*

The country's excellent healthcare facilities and low cost of living have helped the country maintain its popularity among retirees from the US and many other parts of the world. Especially with its high quality of life and the unique, vibrant culture.

#9 - *Costa Rica*

A country famed for its outdoor activities, Costa Rica offers retirees low-cost real estate, friendly locals and an affordable way of life. These qualities and more have kept this country a favorite retirement destination for years.

#10 - *Panama*

Low cost of living, great weather, wonderfully friendly locals and low tax burden have all made Panama a long-time favorite with retirees looking to settle abroad. The country's Pensionado Program affords eligible individuals a chance to enjoy many of the numerous benefits afforded in the program, such as a discount on certain medical expenses.

Buying a Vacation Home Without Any Savings

Realistically, it is nearly impossible to purchase a home if you don't have a lot of money saved up. Especially given how expensive houses are these days. The American Dream of owning a home is one that lives on in the hearts of many, despite the rising costs, but if you don't have any money saved, what could you do about it?

Relocating to somewhere cheaper would be the first step. If you can't afford a home where you currently live, you're going to have to go elsewhere. You need to choose your location very carefully, and then compare that with how much you could afford to spend. Buying a home *may* still be possible even if you have little to no money saved up, but you're going to have to plan your steps carefully as you go about it.

- **You Need to Buy Below Budget -** This is one way of affording a home, to buy one that is under your budget so you avoid straining yourself far too much financially. It may not be exactly what you hoped and dream, but if you believe it's still better than not owning any kind of home at all, minimize your financial stress by buying something that is under your budget.

- **Being Realistic About Usage -** Especially if it's a vacation home. How often do you plan to use it? If it's only going to be for a few weeks in a year, then shelling out a fortune on something you can't afford doesn't make good financial sense. Go back to buying under budget to make it a win-win situation. Or better still rent it as we discuss below.

- **Remember the Tax Implications -** Don't forget about the property taxes that come with owning a home.

- **Renting Out Your Vacation Home** - Consider renting out your vacation home when you're not using it which may enable you to afford another home and mortgage.

Is It Possible to Make $100,000 to $250,000 In My Retirement?

It is, and the way to do it is through entrepreneurship. Let's face it; if you're no longer making a steady paycheck, chances are coming into that kind of money is going to be almost impossible, especially if you haven't saved up for it. Many retirees today are taking that leap of faith and taking their chances venturing into generating passive income or creating an online business. In Chapter 1, we talked about how it was never too late to start going after your dreams, drawing inspiration from Colonel Sanders and Grandma Moses, who found success well after the hit the retirement age.

In Chapter 3 and 4, we talked about how to turn your passion into your professions, and how running an online business could be done as long as you were willing to learn with a determined drive to succeed. Here are even more inspiring, everyday individuals like you and me who are living proof of the advice you've been reading about in the past few chapters *can work* for you if you're willing to leave your excuses at the door and take a leap of faith.

- **Jim Butenschoen** - Started a hair design company called the Career Academy of Hair Design at 65.

- **Rand Smith -** Started an optical retail business in his 50s by tapping into his retirement funds with his wife. He owns the Smith Sport & Fashion Optical store.

- **Chris and Susan Beesley -** Started an online business in their mid-50s knowing nothing except the basics about the online world. They now run their blog chrisandsusanbeesley.com, an online business education site dedicated to helping entrepreneurs.

- **Michael Grottola -** Started a consulting firm at 65 helping new businesses get access to the capital that they need for their start up.

- **Colin King -** Started Education Quizzes in his 50s, an online business providing educational quizzes for school-aged kids.

- **Angie Higa -** Launched a travel blanket manufacturing company called Sky Dreams in 2009 after retiring early in 2008.

- **Marcia Duhart -** Started her business at 50 by founding CyberSenior Services, teaching retirees and the elderly who want to learn computer skills.

- **Radha Daga -** Founded Triguni Foods at the age of 73.

Think you've got no money to invest in starting an online business? Think again, because you *don't* need a lot of capital to start some great these days. With as little as $0, $100 or $1000, the following businesses will cost you next to nothing to get started (well, except the cost of the website of course):

- Consulting will cost you almost nothing to get started offering your skills and expertise.
- Pet sitting businesses
- Online tutoring
- Translation services
- Travel guide services for your local area
- Home cooked meals business
- Babysitting
- Professional organizer
- Photography or editing services
- Wedding or event planner

Bonus Savings Hack: Lowering Your Taxes in Retirement

Another savings hack to help you cut cost in your retirement years is to find ways of lowering the taxes you're slapped with in retirement. With some savvy tax planning, you could be looking at paying a lot less tax between 55 and 70 through the following strategies:

- Keep your savings in tax-deferred retirement accounts, like your 401(K) and IRA.
- Know your tax bracket threshold and take note of the cut-off points using your filing status.
- Stay in the lower tax bracket by

keeping your monthly expenses low so you end up withdrawing less from your retirement accounts.

• Opt to live in states which are tax-friendly for retirees, like Florida.

• Roll your IRA over to a Health Savings Account (HSA) if you've got a high-deductible health insurance plan.

• Consider making charitable contributions directly from the required minimum distribution amount to receive tax benefits. This can still be done even without itemizing.

Chapter 9: How to Travel the World in Your Retirement

Hans Christian Anderson summed it up perfectly when he said *to travel is to live*. Those five little words alone explain why traveling the world is a dream for both the young and old, and those who did not get to do so much of it while they were busy working when they're younger now want to do it after they retire. After all, there's so much of the world to see and now that they've entered the next phase of their life, leaving the 9-5 world behind, what better way to spend their time than to explore everywhere they wanted to go?

Traveling in your retirement years may just be more affordable than you think, and you don't even need a fortune to get it done if you travel hack just right. Domestically or internationally, with careful planning, you could travel the world for less money by reducing your travel cost whenever possible, taking advantage of air miles and other various ongoing promotions, even by using the right time to search for flights.

Depending on where you go, not every country in the world is going to cost a fortune for you to visit. Countries with a lower cost of living means you're able to keep your expenses low, and you could consider starting off in those countries while saving up for the more expensive places. Among the cheapest countries in the world are:

- Nicaragua
- Laos
- Turkey
- Cambodia
- Thailand
- India
- Nepal
- Indonesia
- Vietnam
- Myanmar
- China
- Malaysia
- Philippines
- Armenia
- Oman
- Bangladesh
- Russia
- Mexico
- Guatemala
- Panama
- Peru
- Chile
- Bolivia
- Ecuador
- Ethiopia
- Morocco
- Egypt
- Estonia
- South Africa
- Lithuania
- Latvia
- Macedonia

- Albania
- Ukraine
- Portugal
- Spain
- Greece

Some of the countries mentioned above are so affordable living on just $30 a day is entirely possible. Traveling abroad is exciting, and once you have a country in mind, it's time to book one of the biggest travel costs incurred. Flight tickets.

Travel Hacks - Booking Cheap Flights
Travel companies and airlines these days know how much people love to travel, and they've done their best to provide options which make traveling today more affordable than ever. Running frequent promotions and special holiday offers has become the norm, with some airlines even offering special vacation deals which could include round trip tickets from Germany to Israel for just $35 with Ryanair. If you book during the right time, you could take advantage of the low fares and promotions being offered and save yourself a lot of money on plane tickets.

When booking your next flight out, try the following travel hacks to save you some much-needed cash:

- **Be Invisible -** A great tip which has been around for some time now is to make yourself "invisible" online when searching for flight tickets. Or at least untraceable. Travel websites and airline companies often show much higher prices when you repeatedly search for flight tickets, something you would have no doubt noticed if you're a frequent flyer. That's because these airline companies rely on a variable pricing system, and adjust air fares based on your search history. A quick trick is to either open a search page in Google's incognito window, or simply turn off your cookies to become untraceable to these companies.

• **One Way Tickets Can Sometimes Be Cheaper** - Instead of jumping in straight away and booking a round-trip ticket immediately, check how much it would cost you to buy a one-way ticket. This could sometimes turn out to be a cheaper option. Keep your options open and if you see a great deal, book it right away because you may not find it again.

• **Buy Your Tickets One at A Time** - Airlines often have one or two tickets available at any given time for the lower price range, and it is recommended that if you're going in a family that you buy your tickets one at a time. Bulk booking can automatically get you bumped to the higher price bracket. Buying tickets one at a time may take longer, but it'll save you more money down the road.

• **The Bigger the Airport, the Cheaper the Fare** - If you didn't already know this, flying out to the bigger airports can be much cheaper than the smaller, less popular ones. New York may be one of the most expensive cities in the world, but its airport is one of the cheapest to fly to in the world too. Aim to fly out to the biggest available airport and then consider taking a bus or train to the city that you want to go to. Getting creative this way with your travel saves a bundle.

• **Setting Up a Fare Monitor -** Google flights, Skyscanner AirfareWatchdog.com, and Hopper as soon as the ticket fare for the destination you've been eyeing has dropped.

• **Sign Up for Alerts -** Consider subscribing to newsletters from travel publications or travel search engines like Travelocity or Expedia. They often produce some pretty amazing deals if you're willing to be flexible with your travels.

• **Have You Heard of <u>Holiday Pirates</u>? -** This website is a new favorite travel hack among many holiday goers looking for the best travel deals and major savings. The website claims to bring its users more than 50,000 deals every year, putting together some of the best deals with the help of over 200 pirates who hail from 33 countries across the globe. The website's team of deal hunters scour the web for the best and cheapest deals, which include flights and hotels and more.

What If I Don't Want to Fly, But *Still* Want to Travel the World?

Since most people are unlikely to hit the $1 million in retirement savings target given the rising cost of living these days, they'll be on the lookout for all the possible alternatives that they have to work with. If buying a vacation home is out of your budget, and spending a lot of time in a cramped economy class cabin isn't quite the perfect solution yet, there's one more option that you got on your table. What about the idea of retiring on a *cruise ship*?

Before you back away with your hands raised in the air because cruise ships are often associated with luxury travel, just hold on for it minute. Yes, they are luxury travel for occasional travelers, but *retiring on a cruise ship* is something else altogether. Working on the basis that you've accumulated less than $1 million for your retirement savings, booking these individual cruises for your travels could be a more realistic approach to go, with a lot of careful planning of course. Especially if you're not rushing to get yourself from one destination to another, cruise ships are the more comfortable way to travel too, especially when you don't have to spend a lot of time cramped in a small plane cabin.

How much you can expect to spend on these cruise ships would depend on the cruise line that you go with and the deal that you manage to get. Princess Cruise Line is one example where if you get lucky, you could end up with fantastic last minute deals, which start at $79 per person daily. If you were hopping on board a 15-day long cruise at that price point, you're looking at spending a base rate amount of $1,185. Now, if you were to book yourself on back-to-back cruises, you could be looking at paying $2,370 per month. Keep your cruise fares consistently low and you've got a good chance of spending less than $30,000 a year, with food, lodging and all the onboard luxuries and facilities available for you to enjoy.

Bonus Tips: Keep Your Fares Low While Cruising

Be warned though that because cruise ships are still catering towards that 'vacation' theme, you will be bombarded with the occasional sales pitches every now and then. Deals could include anything from massages, souvenirs, alcoholic beverages and shore excursions, all tempting you to spend some extra cash for these additional treats. If you want to stand firm on the strict budget you have set for yourself, here are a couple of good tips to stretch out your dollars and keep your expenses low while cruising the seven seas:

- Skip on splurging on those specialty restaurants and opt to eat in the free dining venues already provided on board the ship as part of the facilities.

- On board spa treatments can be expensive, so skip out on those and save your spa appointments for port days instead.

- Be careful not to over tip, there's no reason to feel pressured to do so.

• Explore on shore on your own and save money on booking tours. Exploring on your own is part of the fun anyway!

• Beverages on board are charged at the same price as restaurants, so if you really want to indulge, opt for the discounted packages or be on the lookout for special offers. Alternatively, consider bringing your own beverages to save even more money.

• The cruise prices don't agree with you, there's no reason to force yourself to make a booking. There'll be other packages, other cruise operators and other deals.

• When you're already on board an existing cruise, there's no reason to rush to book your next one. Cruise prices are much higher when booking on board, despite the packages and perks which are being touted to you. Sometimes paying for little extras separately could work out to be cheaper overall.

• Consider booking excursions onshore which are outside the cruise line. Many tourist destinations have local tour package offerings which could work out to be cheaper.

• Avoid the temptation to buy beverage packages on the very first day. When you purchase a package, you're buying it for the entirety of your cruise. Which means if your cruise is 7-days long, you're paying for the entire 7-days. Wait a couple of days if it's not necessary and save yourself some cash.

• Even when at port, opt to eat on board instead. After all, you did pay for the food already as part of your package.

• If you intend to spend a lot of time cruising, it might be worth looking into joining the customer loyalty program offered by the cruise line.

• Shopping on board can be costly, so give it a miss if the items can still be found on land for much cheaper.

When Cruising Becomes Your Life

Some retirees love being on board cruise ships so much that they've made it their full-time retirement. Mama Lee Wachstetter is one example, and she's become a household name on Crystal Cruises, and she's been living on board the Crystal Serenity for the past 9 years. She loved it so much she even wrote a book about her experience entitled ***I May Be Homeless But You Should See My Yacht,*** which is available for purchase on Amazon. How is she affording this lifestyle? By paying Crystal Cruises every six months, which affords her bigger discounts.

Vancouver couple Jack and Willi Ross traded in their single-family home in exchange for a smaller apartment and a chance to travel more. This trade-off enabled them to indulge in month-long cruises and the occasional 180-day voyages onboard Oceania Cruises. The Ross' even told **CNBC** that the cost of living was much cheaper in some ways compared to living at home.

Oceania Cruises and many others have revealed that more retirees are cruising now compared to several years ago. A study conducted based on the life span of 20-years, cruise ships were found to be evenly matched price wise when compared to assisted living centers. They were, in fact, more efficacious, the study revealed, published in the Journal of American Geriatrics Society. It was noted that the cost of living on land did vary significantly, depending on where you lived and what your needs were.

Chapter 10: BONUS 5 ways to invest $100

Well done, you! You've made it this far and hopefully come to realize that even if your savings doesn't seem like it's enough, you can still crush it in retirement and live your dreams. The life you have *always* wanted it still possible! In this final chapter, we'll take a look at even *more* ways in which you could invest as little as $100 to make something happen.

$100 may not seem like a lot, but the key to investing is *time*. Over time, that amount can grow to something big. If an 18-year old were to invest at least $100 per month with interest averaging 7% approximately, by the time you hit 38, you would have accumulated more than $40k over that time. You don't have to be 18-years old to begin because anytime is a good time to start investing, even if you've already retired. It's never too late because wealth accumulation is an ongoing process, and if you don't use that money, you could always leave it behind for your next of kin.

Let's take a look at the five extra ways in which you could invest $100 wisely.

Investment Strategy #1 - Cryptocurrency
If you've been playing around with the idea of investing in cryptocurrency for a while now, **Coin Market Cap** is a website which makes it easy for you to identify the most popular cryptocurrencies on the market. To make a

purchase, all you would need to do is check the corresponding page and determine in which markets these currencies were traded. Cryptocurrencies are best described as a form of distributed digital currency. Sort of like the digital cash you have stored in your PayPal accounts.

The benefits that come with cryptocurrencies are the seamless, very fast, and direct transactions between the involved parties. Plus, you have complete control over your balance and your payments, which means that you can earn and spend with transparency. It also eliminates the need for having a central authority validate your transactions too since it all goes through the cryptocurrency network. There are no banks or credit card providers acting as gatekeepers for your money. BitCoin, Ethereum, LiteCoin are just some of the many examples of cryptocurrencies available. As you can see on Coin Market Cap, there are a lot more options available and you could source one that is within your budget if you're thinking about getting into the game.

Investment Strategy #2 - Online Courses
Investing in your own education is always worth it, and if you've got $100 to spare, there are plenty of online courses available where you could build on your existing skills and knowledge. Online courses in various subjects are aplenty, and they are a convenient, sometimes even cheaper alternative than enrolling into a full-time program at a traditional university. The advantage of online courses is that you can learn anytime, anywhere and from the comfort of your own home. The skills you learn could certainly be put to good use, especially if you're running a business in your retirement years. All you need is a passion for

learning, a drive to succeed and a $100 to invest in your future.

Investment Strategy #3 - Betterment

Ever heard of **Betterment**? Probably not until you started seriously researching investment options. Well, now that you're ready to get started, Betterment can be a great entry point to those who are new in the investment world. A robo-advisor online software designed to help you better manage your investments, Betterment uses algorithms which are computer-generated to help you make the best investment decisions. Yes, there is no human equation in this mix, everything is completely automated and fully computerized. Welcome to the future of investment. Using robo-advisors technology is exactly how platforms like Betterment are able to keep their fees much, much lower than what you would have to pay if you were to engage the services of a financial advisor who was there to actively manage your funds.

Since it was founded in 2008, Betterment has now grown to become one of the largest robo-advisor investment brokerage platforms out there. Platforms like these work on the philosophy that *everyone* can invest, and why not when Betterment has no minimum spend amount required to open an account to get started? The investment fee you get is also at a significantly lower cost than traditional investment methods. If your account holds between $0 - $10,000 and you made an auto-deposit of $100 monthly, the fee you would be charged is 0.25%. Autho-deposit is highly recommended with this one, so you never miss a month (unless you only intend to deposit when you've got

$100 to spare). If you're looking for a simple way of investing, Betterment could be the online platform for you.

Investment Strategy #4 - Ally Invest

If Betterment isn't your cup of tea, or even if you're looking for another option to diversify your investments, take a look at **Ally Invest**. Formerly known as TradeKing, Ally Invest is a platform which offers its users diversified financial services. It doesn't just do trading, it offers lending and banking too, given that the company's main focus is to provide its users with tools which are easy and convenient to use and priced at an affordable range. Among the pros that come with Ally Invest include a good selection of tools that to help you find and execute your trading options, the available banking capabilities which have been integrated into the investment experience, and its customizable InvestLIVE platform which provides the option of streaming quotes. The website, however, can be a little difficult and tricky to navigate until you get used to it.

Ally Invest targets its services towards investors who hover around the entry level to intermediate range, and investors who are keen on having their investments in closer proximity to their banking accounts. If this sounds like something you could be keen on putting your $100 into, then it might be worth looking into if you want more diversification for your money.

Investment Strategy #5 - Peer-to-Peer Lending

This is a system where people who have the money to *invest* are matched with people who are looking to take a loan. Also known as marketplace lending, peer-to-peer lending (P2P lending) usually takes place on a website or online platform of some sort, where borrowers and lenders can come together for a mutual reason. The P2P system provides an alternative for those who are not looking to go through the usual lender routes (banks, credit unions, building societies, etc), for a personal or business loan that they might need. Investors who have the cash to spare come to the rescue and the borrowers repay the loan over time with interest (of course). The platform serves as a legitimate intermediary between the borrowers and the investors, and the platform makes its money by charging *both* parties with fees. If you've got $100 to invest in starting, you could consider becoming an investor for those seeking a small loan. You'll gain a little bit of interest with that small investment.

Conclusion

Thank for making it through to the end of this book, let's hope it was informative and able to provide you with all of the tools you need to achieve your goals whatever they may be.

There is absolutely no reason why you cannot enjoy your golden years and live the life that you want. If you are already retired and do not have enough savings, please know there is still time. *It's never too late unless you stop trying.* Don't allow fear to get in the way of your retirement dream because as we have explored, there are plenty of ways to stretch your retirement dollars to generate income.

Benjamin Franklin once said, "If you fail to plan, you plan to fail." Begin taking small steps by making the most out of your skills, knowledge and network you've gained throughout your working years, and turn them into something that can build your retirement fund. Skills, knowledge, and talent *will never* expire until you allow them to, and since you've spent most of your lifetime building them, let them work for you now. Set up a plan, use our guide and follow the steps. Remember that all things take time and effort to build. Don't be bogged down by defeating thoughts. Celebrate quick wins and keep at it until it yields results. It is never too late until you say it is.

Finally, if you found this book useful in anyway, a review on Amazon is always appreciated!

Afterward

As you look forward at the years of retirement ahead of you, you know that you should be happy. Celebrating that this is finally the time to live out all those dreams you've had to put aside for years due to work commitments.

But you can't stop the beads of anxious sweat from dripping down your forehead as one alarming thought continues to linger in your mind.

I don't have enough savings for my retirement.

The challenges of retiring with zero savings may seem insurmountable without having a solid plan, but that doesn't mean we should be giving up our retirement dream just yet. Sarah Carter Crews and her husband are living proof that even if you retire without having enough savings, life doesn't have to be a dead end, and that *is it still possible* for you to create a passive income stream steady enough to ease your financial worries. Retirement is a time that is meant to be enjoyed, to fulfill all those bucket list dreams you've held onto for years, and they are going to show you just how to do it.

Is it possible to survive retirement with absolutely no savings? **Yes and no**.

Yes - If you are committed to step out and follow a well-crafted plan, and stick to it.

No - If you are planning to sit back and do nothing about your depleting finances, thinking that everyone else is in the same boat.

Retirement Income Strategy If Financial Planning Is Not Enough is going explore the many ways you can earn passive or residual income while you enjoy your retirement with your friends and family. This isn't going to be just another motivational book that will encourage you on your way to financial freedom. This is the practical, step-by-step roadmap that you have been searching for all along that is going to walk you down the path towards following your retirement dreams.

This book is going to demonstrate just how easy it is for *everyone* no matter what their financial status may be, can begin taking control of their finances today. Whether you're retired or planning to retire, you *don't have to give up on your retirement dreams just yet.* Not just yet. It's time to take retirement into your own hands.

Bibliography : Retirement Income Strategy If Financial Planning is Not Enough

By

Retirement Reimagination Academy

Chapter 1 Sources
• https://www.daveramsey.com/blog/can-you-retire-on-1-million
• http://longevity.stanford.edu/sightlines-financial-security-special-report-mobile/
• https://www.gobankingrates.com/saving-money/savings-advice/half- americans-less-savings-2017/
• https://www.foxbusiness.com/personal-finance/heres-how-long-1-million-in- retirement-savings-will-last-in-your-state
• https://www.cnbc.com/2018/08/06/how-long-1-million-lasts-in-retirement.html
• http://www.interest.com/savings/news/see-how-well-prepared-retirement-4- rule/
• https://www.investopedia.com/articles/retirement/08/retire-on-1-million- dollars.asp
• https://www.foxbusiness.com/personal-finance/the-new-retirement-mindset

Chapter 2 Sources
• https://www.gobankingrates.com/
• https://www.ssa.gov/news/press/factsheets/basicfact-alt.pdf
• https://www.gao.gov/assets/690/681722.pdf
• https://www.psychologytoday.com/us/blog/the-science-behind-behavior/201611/4-different-ways-think-retirement
• https://www.businessinsider.com/prepare-for-retirement-through-visualization- 2011-4?IR=T

• https://www.chrishogan360.com/4-easy-ways-to-visualize-your-retirement- goals/
• https://www.thenational.ae/business/money/visualise-your-future-to-get-your- retirement-plan-on-track-1.884518
• https://www.americanexpress.com/en-us/business/trends-and-insights/articles/5-ways-to-find-your-hidden-talents/
• https://www.inc.com/leonard-kim/how-to-discover-the-hidden-talents-that-will- make-you-a-business-star.html
• http://www.willpowered.co/learn/discover-passion-ability-and-value
• https://www.careeraddict.com/find-your-talent
• https://www.aconsciousrethink.com/9149/find-your-talents/
• https://personal.vanguard.com/us/insights/retirement/saving/set-retirement- goals
• https://www.imoney.my/articles/guide-retirement-goals
• https://www.thebalance.com/goals-to-help-you-save-for-retirement-2386375
• https://www.regions.com/Insights/Personal/Retirement/ Establishing-a- plan/Planning-for-Retirement-How-to-Set-Retirement-Savings-Goals
• https://www.newretirement.com/retirement/6-meaningful-ways-to-leave-a- financial-legacy-to-your-heirs/
• https://www.chrishogan360.com/what-financial-legacy-are-you-leaving- behind/
• https://www.mutualofomaha.com/advice/tackle-my-finances/how-to-leave-a- financial-legacy-when-you-arent-wealthy
• https://www.newretirement.com/retirement/6-meaningful-ways-to-leave-a- financial-legacy-to-your-heirs/
• https://www.forbes.com/sites/garrettgunderson/2016/06/24/the-successful- entrepreneurs-guide-to-leaving-a-financial-legacy-that-wont-spoil-your- kids/#7133b1695ca9

Chapter 3 Sources

• https://www.entrepreneur.com/article/297899
• https://www.forbes.com/sites/chicceo/2012/10/04/10-things-to-consider-when- starting-a-business-in-a-down-economy/#15e81da46ea3
• https://drivinginnovation.ie.edu/6-things-to-consider-before-starting-business/
• https://www.businessnewsdaily.com/1484-starting-a-business.html
• https://startups.co.uk/7-important-factors-to-consider-before-starting-a- business/
• http://www.smarta.com/advice/starting-up/starting-your-own-business/21- things-to-research-before-starting-a-business/index.html
• https://mpm.ph/before-starting-a-business/
• https://www.pluralsight.com/blog/career/tips-for-marketing-yourself-as-a- freelancer
• https://smallbiztrends.com/2018/07/ways-a-freelancer-can-market- themselves.html
• https://www.outbrain.com/help/advertisers/freelancer-marketing/
• https://www.socialmediatoday.com/social-networks/2015-04-08/13-ways-use- facebook-personal-branding
• https://www.postplanner.com/tips-for-branding-yourself-on-facebook/
• https://www.marketingsherpa.com/article/how-to/how-to-market-yourself-your
• https://thewriteconversation.blogspot.com/2011/09/top-10-ways-to-promote- yourself-on.html
• https://www.businessnewsdaily.com/5453-how-to-promote-your-small- business-on-facebook.html
• https://blog.wishpond.com/post/44154872444/infographic-the-impact-of- photos-on-facebook
• https://www.onblastblog.com/get-instafamous-how-to-market-yourself-on- instagram/

- https://sproutsocial.com/insights/promote-your-instagram/
- https://99designs.com/blog/business/instagram-marketing/
- https://later.com/blog/brand-yourself-on-instagram/
- https://blog.depositphotos.com/how-to-market-yourself-on-instagram.html
- https://www.entrepreneur.com/article/280964
- https://sellers.fiverr.com/en/article/top-10-tips-for-new-fiverr-sellers
- https://blog.fiverr.com/market-yourself-freelance/
- https://thefreelanceeffect.com/make-money-fiverr/
- https://sidehustleacademy.com/udemy-vs-teachable/
- https://krystalwascher.com/blog-bloggers-course-creators/udemy-vs- teachable-for-creating-online-courses
- https://thedigitalmerchant.com/course-platforms/thinkific-vs-udemy-vs- teachable-which-is-best-for-online-course-creators/
- https://www.aaronward.com/blog/teachable-vs-udemy
- https://www.udemy.com/create-your-online-course-creation-platform-with- teachable/

Chapter 4 Sources
- https://jerichowriters.com/self-publish-book-amazon-kindle-kdp/
- https://www.copyblogger.com/how-to-publish-kindle-ebook/
- https://www.sallyannmiller.com/ultimate-guide-to-self-publishing/
- https://self-publishingschool.com/self-publishing-on-amazon/
- https://kindlepreneur.com/how-to-start-a-publishing-company/
- https://blog.hubspot.com/marketing/publishing
- https://www.shopify.my/guides/dropshipping
- https://www.sitegiant.my/the-ultimate-guide-to-dropshipping-what-you-should- know/
- https://www.salehoo.com/dropship
- https://crazylister.com/blog/dropshipping-guide-success-story/
- https://www.acx.com/
- https://www.lulu.com/

Chapter 5 Sources

- https://learnairbnb.com/airbnb-hosting-beginners-guide/
- https://www.goatsontheroad.com/air-bnb-host/
- https://www.swedishnomad.com/airbnb-guide/
- https://medium.com/our-future/the-ultimate-airbnb-hosting-guide- f1f908318551
- https://fouraroundtheworld.com/the-complete-beginners-guide-to-airbnb/
- https://optimizemybnb.com/definitive-guide-airbnb-plus/
- https://gigworker.com/airbnb-vs-homeaway/
- https://www.mymillennialguide.com/airbnb-hosting-beginners-guide/
- https://www.airdna.co/
- https://www.fundera.com/blog/becoming-an-airbnb-host
- https://www.travelandleisure.com/hotels-resorts/vacation-rentals/how-to-be- an-airbnb-host
- https://thepointsguy.com/2017/07/how-to-be-a-great-airbnb-host/
- https://learnairbnb.com/airbnb-hosting-beginners-guide/
- https://www.buzzfeed.com/anniedaly/pro-tips-from-airbnb-superhosts
- https://www.airbnb.com/help/article/39/what-factors-determine-how-my-listing- appears-in-search-results
- https://www.guesty.com/blog/step-by-step-guide-how-to-list-on-airbnb/
- https://help.homeaway.com/articles/How-do-I-list-my-property-HA
- https://www.lodgify.com/blog/optimize-homeaway-listing/
- https://www.lodgify.com/vacation-rental-guide/homeaway/fees/
- https://www.airdna.co/blog/homeaway-vs-vrbo-where-should-you-list
- https://www.syncbnb.com/guides/how-to-create-a-listing-on-homeaway/
- https://championtraveler.com/news/how-to-list-rent-your-place-on-vrbo-for- free/

• https://www.lodgify.com/blog/optimize-vrbo-listing/
• https://www.today.com/series/things-i-wish-i-knew/things-know-listing-airbnb- vrbo-t112818
• https://www.mumsmakelists.com/easy-ways-to-sell-clutter/
• https://www.thriftyfrugalmom.com/7-ways-make-money-selling-clutter/
• https://www.decluttr.com/
• https://www.abebooks.com/

Chapter 6 Sources
• https://blog.hubspot.com/marketing/facebook-paid-ad-checklist
• https://intellifluence.com/blog/why-social-media-marketing-matters
• https://blog.hubspot.com/marketing/social-media-frequency-industry- benchmarks
• https://www.bluecorona.com/blog/social-media-marketing-matter-small- businesses
• https://www.wordtracker.com/academy/social/getting-started/why-social- media-matters
• https://www.contentfac.com/9-reasons-social-media-marketing-should-top- your-to-do-list/
• https://blog.hubspot.com/marketing/social-media-marketing
• https://sproutsocial.com/insights/social-media-marketing-strategy/
• https://blog.hootsuite.com/how-to-create-a-social-media-marketing-plan/
• https://buffer.com/library/social-media-marketing-strategy
• https://neilpatel.com/what-is-social-media-marketing/

Chapter 7 Sources
• https://www.payingforcare.org/lasting-power-of-attorney/
• http://www.attwoodandco.co.uk/fundamental-differences-between-ordinary- and-lasting-power-of-attorney/
• https://uk.practicallaw.thomsonreuters.com/7-382-6293?transitionType=Default&contextData=(sc.Default)&firstPa

ge=true&bhcp=1
- https://www.elderlawanswers.com/powers-of-attorney-come-in-different- flavors-8217
- https://uslegal.com/powerofattorney/
- https://www.lawdepot.com/law-library/faq/power-of-attorney-faq-united- states/#.XSgBGpMzbjA
- https://help.legalnature.com/articles/what-are-the-types-of-powers-of-attorney- and-what-are-the-differences
- https://www.notarize.com/blog/types-of-power-of-attorney
- https://www.legalzoom.com/articles/what-is-a-power-of-attorney
- https://www.investopedia.com/terms/p/powerofattorney.asp
- https://www.fmins.com/blog/11-tips-preparing-last-will-testament/
- https://www.self.com/story/things-you-should-do-now-to-prepare-for-your- own-funeral
- https://www.funeralwise.com/plan/how_to/
- https://www.lhlic.com/consumer-resources/average-funeral-cost/
- https://brandongaille.com/37-funeral-industry-statistics-and-trends/
- https://www.thebalance.com/how-to-minimize-death-taxes-3505688
- https://www.estateplanning.com/Understanding-Estate-Taxes/
- https://www.investopedia.com/terms/e/estatetax.asp
- https://www.aginginplace.org/the-complete-guide-to-long-term-care- insurance-for-retirement-planning/
- https://www.investopedia.com/articles/05/031005.asp

Chapter 8 Sources
- https://realestate.usnews.com/places/methodology
- https://money.usnews.com/money/retirement/slideshows/the-best-places-to- retire
- https://www.cnbc.com/2019/03/21/top-10-us-southern-cities-for- retirement.html

• https://www.forbes.com/sites/williampbarrett/2019/04/23/the-best-places-to- retire-in-2019/#316eb5e25c5a
• https://internationalliving.com/the-best-places-to-retire/
• https://www.forbes.com/sites/nextavenue/2019/01/04/the-top-10-places-in- the-world-to-retire-2-new-lists/#5e20f34956bc
• https://money.usnews.com/money/retirement/baby-boomers/slideshows/the- best-affordable-places-to-retire-overseas
• https://www.telegraph.co.uk/finance/personalfinance/pensions/9677415/The- 10-best-places-to-retire-abroad.html
• https://www.investopedia.com/financial-edge/0611/how-to-afford-a-second- home.aspx
• https://www.daveramsey.com/blog/afford-vacation-home
• https://moneywise.com/a/can-you-afford-a-vacation-home
• https://www.forbes.com/sites/taramastroeni/2018/09/26/thinking-of-buying-a- vacation-home-ask-yourself-these-4-financial-questions-first/#11822cd7261b
• https://smartasset.com/investing/how-to-buy-a-second-home
• https://wellkeptwallet.com/buy-a-home-without-mortgage/
• https://www.fool.com/retirement/2018/11/14/can-you-retire-on-250000-a- survey-says-39-of-ameri.aspx
• https://www.thebalance.com/what-s-your-retirement-number-453995
• https://arkenea.com/blog/entrepreneurs-above-50/
• https://blog.taxact.com/6-steps-to-minimizing-taxes-on-retirement-income/
• https://www.marketwatch.com/story/7-ways-to-reduce-taxes-in-retirement- 2019-04-08
• https://www.cnbc.com/2018/11/01/6-ways-to-cut-retirement-tax-surprises.html
• https://www.fool.com/investing/2019/03/02/2-strategies-to-reduce-your-taxes- in-retirement.aspx

Chapter 9 Sources

- https://www.cruisecritic.com/articles.cfm?ID=1096
- https://www.cruisecritic.com/articles.cfm?ID=1096
- https://www.investopedia.com/articles/retirement/101416/how-retire-cruise- ship-less-1-million.asp
- https://www.forbes.com/sites/debbikickham/2018/04/23/how-to-retire-on-a- luxury-cruise-ship/#7e98a8f513f5
- https://thriftynomads.com/booking-cheapest-flight-possible-anywhere/
- https://www.nomadicmatt.com/travel-tips/how-to-find-a-cheap-flight/
- https://www.businessinsider.com/23-secrets-to-booking-cheap-flights-2012- 7?IR=T
- https://www.skyscanner.net/news/expert-tips-for-snagging-a-cheap-flight
- https://smartasset.com/retirement/cheapest-countries-to-retire
- https://www.investopedia.com/articles/retirement/042116 /worlds-cheapest- safest-retirement-countries.asp
- https://internationalliving.com/the-best-places-to-retire/
- https://www.goabroad.com/articles/jobs-abroad/cheapest-countries-live-and- work
- https://www.gobankingrates.com/saving-money/home/cheapest-countries-to- live-in/
- •https://www.holidaypirates.com/tourism/providers/about-us/
- https://www.amazon.com/May-Homeless-But-Should-Yacht/dp/0692932569/ref=sr_1_1?ie=UTF8&qid=1524586329&sr=8-1&keywords=mama+lee&dpID=51O7woa54TL&preST=_SY34 4_BO1,204,203,200_QL70_&dpSrc=srch
- https://www.cnbc.com/2017/03/24/cruise-ships-are-the-new-snowbirding- paradise.html

Chapter 10 Sources

• https://moneycheck.com/ally-invest-review/
• https://www.ally.com/do-it-right/investing/investing-in-stocks-a-beginners- guide-part-1-an-introduction/
• https://investorjunkie.com/investing/should-you-take-online-courses/
• https://investingsimple.blog/beginners-guide-to-betterment-robo-advisor/
• https://www.ally.com/invest/
• https://investingsimple.blog/beginners-guide-to-betterment-robo-advisor/
•https://www.betterment.com/?utm_campaign=General_Aff_LP &utm_med ium=affiliate&utm_source=Listen%20Money%20Matters% 20LLC&o ffer_campaign_id=1c8d4070-1003-4bb0-a4c5-35b3a3a9cf51&clickid=QoSzPc14MxyJUsM0GIyI522MUk lzq9TB9SY5X E0&dclid=CjkKEQjwtMvlBRCPpsDxuZSyp64BEiQAay4p lJkEs4htaRcj1dr l-6GddDjgFg0Qi_wwKs0M3vmu9WLw_wcB
• https://coinmarketcap.com/
• https://cryptominded.com/starters-guide-cryptocurrencies/
• https://coinsutra.com/cryptocurrency-investing/
• https://masterthecrypto.com/crypto-guides-for-beginners/
•https://www.forbes.com/sites/robertberger/2015/11/06/an-investors-guide-to- peer-to-peer-lending/#62bed25a60e5
•https://www.financiallyindependentmom.com/ultimate-guide-p2p-lending/
• https://www.moneywise.co.uk/investing/peer-peer-lending/guide-peer-peer- lending